THE GEOGRAPHICAL CONCEPTIONS
OF COLUMBUS

THE GEOGRAPHICAL CONCEPTIONS
OF
COLUMBUS
A Critical Consideration of Four Problems

by

GEORGE E. NUNN

Expanded Edition

with a new essay

"The Test of Time"

by

CLINTON R. EDWARDS

The American Geographical Society Collection
of the Golda Meir Library
The University of Wisconsin-Milwaukee
in cooperation with
The American Geographical Society
New York

Expanded Edition
Published 1992
in cooperation with the American Geographical Society, New York
by
The American Geographical Society Collection
of the Golda Meir Library
The University of Wisconsin-Milwaukee
Milwaukee, Wisconsin 53201
Printed in the United States of America

Original edition published in 1924 as no. 14
of the American Geographical Society Research Series
and reprinted in 1972 and 1977.

Expanded edition, 1992
supported by funds from
The International Geographical Congress

Nunn, George E., 1882-
      The geographical conceptions of Columbus: a critical
consideration of four problems / George E. Nunn. —
Expanded ed. / with a new essay "The test of time" by Clinton
R. Edwards.
      p. cm. — (American Geographical Society research
series; no. 14)
      Includes bibliographical references and index.
      1. Columbus, Christopher—Knowledge—Geography.
      2. Geography—15th-16th centuries. 3. Maps, Early.
      I. Edwards, Clinton R. II. Title. III. Series.
E118.N96 1992
970.01'5—dc20   92-71996

ISBN 1-879281-06-6

PREFACE

The Geographical Conceptions of Columbus by George E. Nunn was first published in 1924 by the American Geographical Society as no. 14 in the Society's Research Series. There could be no more appropriate time to reissue this important work than the 500th anniversary of the first voyages of Christopher Columbus.

Discussions on a cooperative venture were held between Mary Lynne Bird, Executive Director of the American Geographical Society in New York City and Peter Watson-Boone, Director of the Golda Meir Library at the University of Wisconsin-Milwaukee, where the American Geographical Society Collection has been housed since 1978. They agreed that the AGS Collection would publish an expanded edition; in addition to a reprint of the original work, it would have a new chapter examining Nunn's theses in the light of subsequent scholarship.

We are very fortunate that Professor Clinton R. Edwards of the University of Wisconsin-Milwaukee Department of Geography accepted the challenge of providing this new chapter. He has done extensive research in cultural and historical geography, especially on early European voyages of discovery, and is an expert on the geography of Latin America. It should also be noted that Dr. Edwards is, himself, a skilled and knowledgable sailor.

The following is a quotation from Edwards' essay, "The Test of Time," which begins on page 151.

> This essay is not intended to be another review of, or an introduction to, *Geographical Conceptions*. Nor is its objective a final judgment concerning the validity of Nunn's conclusions. Rather, it is an attempt to trace the

course of his arguments in his own later contributions and in the hands of other scholars, and to determine to what extent we are closer to answers, building upon his work. Since the essay deals with the subsequent explication of the various theses presented by Nunn, I recommend that his text be read first.

We gratefully acknowledge the support of the International Geographical Congress in producing this expanded edition of *The Geographical Conceptions of Columbus*. It is a fitting commemoration of the quincentennial year of Columbus' discoveries. It is also a substantive example of the creative cooperation between two institutions which share both an illustrious past and a vision of the future - The American Geographical Society and the American Geographical Society Collection at the University of Wisconsin-Milwaukee.

Dr. Roman Drazniowsky, Curator
The American Geographical Society Collection

CONTENTS

AMERICAN GEOGRAPHICAL SOCIETY

RESEARCH SERIES NO. 14

W. L. G. JOERG, *Editor*

THE GEOGRAPHICAL CONCEPTIONS OF COLUMBUS

A Critical Consideration of Four Problems

BY

GEORGE E. NUNN

AMERICAN GEOGRAPHICAL SOCIETY

BROADWAY AT 156TH STREET

NEW YORK

1924

PL.   PLATES

THE DETERMINATION OF THE LENGTH OF A TERRESTRIAL DEGREE BY COLUMBUS

One of the essential questions which Christopher Columbus was called upon to face in formulating his project for a westward voyage was that of the distance to be traversed between Europe and Asia. The circumference of the globe being taken as 360°, the problem resolved itself into (1) the calculation of the length of a degree and (2) an estimate of the extension of Asia eastward. The present study is a discussion of the ideas of Columbus on these two points.

CALCULATION OF THE LENGTH OF A DEGREE

As is well known, Columbus took the length of a degree to be 56⅔ Italian nautical miles.[1] This erroneous figure was not original with him; in fact, it was a commonplace of medieval geography and goes back to the ninth century of our era, when the astronomers of the Caliph Al-Mamûn determined this value for the degree as a result of their historic survey on the plains of Sinjar.[2] In the time of Columbus the estimate of 56⅔ miles was commonly associ-

[1] See the section "The Statements of Columbus," pp. 6–11, below. On the length of the Italian nautical mile see pp. 17–18, below.

[2] J. T. Reinaud and Stanislas Guyard, transls.: Géographie d'Aboulféda, traduite de l'arabe en français, 2 vols. in three, Paris, 1848–83; reference in Vol. 1 (Introduction), pp. cclxix-cclxxiii.

ated with the name of the Arab geographer Al-Far-ghani, known to Western Europe as Alfraganus. The question for consideration here does not concern either the origin or the currency of the figure given; it arises from the statement of Columbus that he had verified the estimate of the 56⅔ miles by deter-mining it himself.[3] The truth of this statement has been called in question by almost every modern critic on the ground that it was practically impossible for Columbus to have made the calculations necessary for the verification. What is implied in this criti-cism is that Columbus had not at his disposal the means elaborated in modern times for the measure-ment of a terrestrial degree; what is overlooked is that Columbus must have carried out his verifica-tion, if at all, by following the accepted practice of his own time.

VIGNAUD'S CRITICISM OF COLUMBUS

As a point of departure we may take the state-ment of Henry Vignaud, the latest writer to discuss the matter in detail. In his "Histoire critique de la grande entreprise de Christophe Colomb" Vignaud says:[4]

Nous arrivons à la plus importante des observations que Colomb dit avoir faites au cours de ses voyages de Guinée: celle qui aurait eu pour résultat la constatation que le degré terrestre ne mesurait, à l'équateur, que

[3] See, below, pp. 9–10, statement VII.
[4] 2 vols., Paris, 1911; reference in Vol. I, pp. 63–67.

56 milles ⅔. Colomb est très affirmatif sur ce point. Il dit qu'à plusieurs reprises il a fait des observations ayant cette détermination pour objet; il assure que des cosmographes du roi de Portugal, envoyés dans ce but, ont constaté l'exactitude de cette mesure de 56 milles ⅔ donnée originairement par l'astronome arabe Alfragan, et il affirme que lui aussi a fait cette vérification. Il n'y a donc ici ni équivoque, ni incertitude; Colomb déclare nettement qu'il a mesuré la longueur du degré équatorial, et que cette longueur est de 56 milles ⅔.

Cette observation diffère de toutes celles que Colomb aurait faites pendant son séjour en Portugal, et qui nous sont données comme l'ayant conduit à la formation de son grand dessein. La constatation que la zone torride, ainsi que la zone glaciale, étaient habitables, le fait que la région équatoriale était très peuplée et toutes les autres observations auxquelles pouvaient donner lieu des voyages aux côtes de Guinée, n'étaient pas de nature à suggérer, même à une imagination ardente, que les Indes et le royaume du Grand Khan devaient se trouver à proximité de la péninsule hispanique. Mais il n'en est pas de même du fait établi scientifiquement que le degré équatorial équivaut à 56 milles ⅔, car ce fait seul contient, en substance, tout le système cosmographique que Colomb a formulé plus tard et sur lequel il dit avoir basé son projet. Si Colomb a fait cette observation, il faut reconnaître que nous sommes ici en présence d'une circonstance qui a pu contribuer à la formation d'un plan ayant pour objet le passage aux Indes par l'ouest.

Mais Colomb a-t-il fait cette observation? Il semble qu'il suffise de poser cette question pour la résoudre. Supposer que Colomb, qui n'avait que des connaissances mathématiques élémentaires, qui ne possédait aucune instruction scientifique, était capable d'entrependre et de mener à bonne fin les opérations savantes nécessaires pour arriver à une détermination, même approximative, de la longueur d'un degré terrestre, c'est méconnaître la valeur des conditions qu'exige la solution d'un tel problème, ou avancer une chose que contredit tout ce que nous savons aujourd'hui de la vie de Colomb.

Il n'est pas nécessaire d'insister davantage sur ce point qui n'est pas controversé. Les critiques les plus autorisés en ces matières ont déclaré, sans hésiter, que Colomb n'était pas capable de faire une opération de ce genre, et ses admirateurs les plus ardents n'ont pas osé s'élever contre cette assertion.

Quelle autre conclusion peut-on tirer de l'exposé qui précède, sinon celle que Colomb s'est attribué un mérite qu'il n'a pas eu, et qu'ici encore, comme dans d'autres circonstances que la critique a relevées, on surprend le grand Génois en flagrant délit d'une de ces inventions auxquelles il se plaisait quelquefois, et qu'on appelle par euphémisme des exagérations, mais qui sont si contraires à la réalité des choses qu'il est difficile de les distinguer de véritables mensonges.

Cette conclusion, suffisamment justifiée par ce qui précède, paraîtra encore plus évidente quand nous montrerons, dans un autre chapitre, où Colomb a pris cette mesure de la Terre qu'il donne pour avoir été vérifiée par lui. Il ne restera alors aucun doute qu'il n'est pas plus exact que Colomb ait mesuré la longueur du degré terrestre, qu'il n'est vrai qu'il ait fait campagne pour le roi René, qu'il comptait des amiraux parmi ses proches, qu'il était d'une famille de marins et qu'il avait navigué toute sa vie, assertions qui viennent toutes de lui, et que l'on sait aujourd'hui être contraires à la vérité.

Ce qu'il faut encore noter ici, c'est que, si l'on écarte des connaissances que Colomb aurait acquises par ses voyages aux côtes d'Afrique, la constatation que le degré équatorial ne valait que 56 milles ⅔, ces voyages ne peuvent avoir exercé aucune influence sur la formation de l'idée qu'il dit avoir toujours été la sienne, que le passage aux Indes par l'ouest était une chose faisable. On conçoit très bien, au contraire, que ces voyages aient eu pour Colomb le résultat indiqué par son fils, celui de lui avoir suggéré la réflexion que, puisque les Portugais avaient pu découvrir de nouvelles terres en s'avançant beaucoup vers le sud, on devait pouvoir en découvrir également en pénétrant plus avant dans les mers de l'ouest.

Vignaud bases his objection, implicitly, upon the assumption that Columbus claimed to have measured the length of some particular degree. This, the present writer agrees, Columbus could not have done with the means at his disposal. Further, it is well known that the estimate of 56⅔ miles was common property long before the time of Columbus. With these two points established, the conclusion is simple: "Colomb s'est attribué un mérite qu'il n'a pas eu," or, as Humboldt gently puts it,[5] he obtained the result "because he knew in advance what he wanted to find." This is the point at which the matter rests.

[5] Alexander von Humboldt: Examen critique de l'histoire de la géographie du nouveau continent et des progrès de l'astronomie nautique aux quinzième et seizième siècles, 5 vols., Paris, 1836–39; reference in Vol. 2, p. 324 (quoted by Vignaud, *op. cit.*, Vol. 1, p. 65, note 97).

Any critical consideration of the problem must begin with the fact that the value of 56⅔ miles for the degree is erroneous and hence could not have been verified by Columbus if there had not been some special factors or elements involved in his mode of procedure. What is of the first importance to observe here is that the information upon which Columbus was forced to rely and the methods followed in his day constitute elements which have hitherto been ignored in the discussion of the problem but which place his claim to have verified the length of a degree in an entirely new light.

THE STATEMENTS OF COLUMBUS

The more important statements of Columbus with reference to the length of a degree are mainly in the form of marginal notes which he had written in his own copies of a universal history and a cosmography current at that time. They are as follows:

I

. . . . quod . . . rex Portugalie misit in Guinea anno Domini .1485. magister Ihosepius, fixicus eius & astrologus, [ad com]piendum altitudinem solis in totta Guinea; qui omnia adinplevit, & renunciavit dito serenissimo regi, me presente, quod . . . alliis in die .xi. marcii invenit se distare ab equinoxiali gradus .v. minute in insula vocata "de los Ydolos," que est prope [sierr]a Lioa. & hoc cum maxima diligencia procuravit. postea vero sepe ditus serenissimus rex misit in Guinea in alliis locis. postea . . . & semper invenit concordari com ipso

magistro Iosepio, quare sertum habeo esse castrum Mine
sub linea equinoxiali.[6] (That . . . the king of Portugal
sent to Guinea, in the year of our Lord 1485, Master Joseph, his physician and astrologer, to ascertain the elevation of the sun in diverse places in Guinea; the said Joseph accomplished this and reported to the said most
serene king, I myself being present, that among other
things on the 11th of March he found that he was distant
from the equator one degree five minutes on an island
called "Los Ydolos," which is near Sierra Leone, and he
made this observation with the very greatest of care.
Moreover, following this, the said most serene king sent
to Guinea in various other places . . . and always he
found agreement with Master Joseph himself. This is
why I hold for certain that the fort of El Mina is on the
equator.)

II

Respondet quolibet gradus miliariis .56⅔., idest .14.
leuce et .23. pasus.[7] (Each degree corresponds to 56⅔
miles, that is 14 leagues and 23 passus.)

III

Nota quod hoc anno de .88., in mense decembri, apu-
lit in Ulixiponam Bartholomeus Didacus, capitaneus
trium caravelarum, quem miserat serenissimus rex Por-
tugallie in Guinea ad tentandum terram; & renunciavit
ipso serenissimo regi prout navigaverit ultra yan naviga-

---

6 Postille alla "Historia rerum ubique gestarum" di Pio II. In: Raccolta di documenti e studi pubblicati dalla R. Commissione Colombiana
pel Quarto Centenario dalla Scoperta dell'America, 6 parts in 14 vols.,
Rome, 1892–96; reference in Part I, Vol. 2, p. 369, No. 860.

7 Postille ai trattati di P. d'Ailly: "Imago Mundi," *ibid.*, Part I, Vol. 2,
p. 374, No. 4.

tum leuche .600., videlicet, .450. ad austrum, et .250. ad aquilonem, usque uno promontorium per ipsum nominatum "cabo de Boa Esperança," quem in Agesinba estimamus; quique in eo loco invenit se distare per astrolabium ultra linea equinociali gradus .45., quem ultimum locum distat ab Ulixbona leuche .3100. quem viagium pictavit & scripsit de leucha in leucha in una carta navigacionis, ut occuli visui ostenderet ipso serenissimo regi. in quibus omnibus interfui.[8] (Note that this year 88, in the month of December, Bartholomew Dias returned to Lisbon, the captain of three caravels, which the most serene king of Portugal had sent to Guinea to discover land; and he reported to that most serene king that he had sailed 600 leagues beyond the farthest region hitherto navigated, namely 450 to the south and 250 to the east, to a cape named by him "Cabo de Boa Esperança," which we think is in Agesinba; and by the astrolabe he found himself in that place to be beyond the equator 45 degrees, which farthest point is distant from Lisbon 3100 leagues. He pictured and wrote down the voyage from league to league in a chart of navigation, that he might show the voyage by eyesight to that most serene king. In all of this I was present.)

IV

Quolibet gradus habet miliaria .56⅔., et sic habet totus circuitus terre .20400.[9] (Each degree has 56⅔ miles, and thus the whole circumference of the earth is 20,400 miles.)

[8] *Ibid.*, pp. 376–377, No. 23.
[9] *Ibid.*, p. 378, No. 28.

V

Actor De spera concordat in latitudine climatum, et non in circuitu terre. Nota quod quolibet gradu equinoxialis realiter respondit miliaria .56⅔.[10] (The author of "De spera" agrees in the latitude of the climates, and not in the circumference of the earth. Note that each degree on the equator really corresponds to 56⅔ miles.)

VI

Nota quod latitudo climatum quem hic videbis, in qua omnes actores concordant, respondet quolibet gradus miliaria .56⅔. & hec est realis, reliqua vero vocalis.[11] (Note that the latitude of the climates which you will see here agrees in all the writers; each degree corresponds to 56⅔ miles. And this is a fact, and whatever anyone says to the contrary is only words.)

VII

Nota quod sepe navigando ex Ulixbona ad austrum in Guinea, notavi cum diligentia viam, ut solent naucleres & malinerios, & postea accepi altitudinem solis cum quadrantem & aliis instrumentis plures vices, & inveni concordare cum Alfragano, videlicet respondere quolibet gradu miliaria .56⅔. quare ad hanc mensuram fidem adhibendam est; igitur posimus dicere quod circuitus terre sub arcu equinociali est .20400. miliaria. similiter quod id invenit magister Yosepius fixicus & astrologus, & alii plures, misi solum ad hoc per serenissimum regem Portugalie, idque potest videre quisquam mentientem per cartas navigationum, mensurando de

10 *Ibid.*, p. 378, No. 30.
11 *Ibid.*, p. 378, No. 31.

septentrione in austro per Occeanum extra omnem terram per lineam rectam, quod bene potest incipiendo in
Anglia vel Hibernia per lineam rectam ad austrum usque
in Guinea.[12] (Note that in sailing frequently from Lisbon to Guinea in a southerly direction, I noted with care
the route followed, according to the custom of pilots and
mariners; and afterward I took the elevation of the sun
many times with quadrant and other instruments, and
I found agreement with Alfraganus, that is to say, each
degree corresponds to 56⅔ miles, wherefore credence
should be given to this measure. Therefore we are able
to say that the circumference of the earth on the equator
is 20,400 miles, likewise that Master Joseph, the physician and astrologer, found this, as did many others sent
solely for this by the most serene king of Portugal; and
anyone can see that there is an error in the navigation
charts by measuring from north to south across the ocean
beyond all land in a straight line, which can easily be
done by starting in England or Ireland with a straight
line to the south as far as Guinea.)

VIII

Unus gradus respondet miliariis .56⅔. et circuitus
terre est leuche .5100. hec est veritas.[13] (One degree
corresponds to 56⅔ miles, and the circumference of the
earth is 5100 leagues. This is the truth.)

IX

El mundo es poco; el injuto d' ello es seis partes, la
séptima sólamente cubierta de agua. la experiençia ia
está vista, i la escriví por otras letras, i con adorna-

---

[12] *Ibid.*, p. 407, No. 490.
[13] *Ibid.*, p. 407, No. 491.

miento de la Sacra Escritura, con el sitio del Paraíso
terrenal que la sancta Iglesia aprueva. digo que el mundo
no es tan grande como diçe el vulgo, i que un grado de
la equinoçial está .56. millas i dos terçios; presto se
tocará con el dedo.[14] (The world is but small; the
dry part of it is six parts, the seventh only is covered
by water. Experience has shown it, and I have discussed
it in other letters, with quotations from the Holy Scripture, with the situation of the terrestrial paradise, which
the Holy Church has approved. I say that the world
is not so large as the common crowd says it is, and that
one degree on the equator is fifty-six miles and two-
thirds. This is a fact that one can touch with one's own
fingers.)

ANALYSIS OF THE STATEMENTS OF COLUMBUS

It will be observed that several of the passages
quoted (II, IV, V, VI, and VIII) are mere reitera-
tions of the assertion that a degree is equal to 56⅔
miles. Quotation III is a note on the Dias expedition to the Cape of Good Hope and is only of incidental value. The last extract, IX, which is from
the letter of July 7, 1503, contains the added information that the world is smaller than popularly supposed;
the notion that six-sevenths of it is dry land is derived from the Books of Esdras.

[14] Letter of July 7, 1503, on the fourth voyage, in Raccolta, Part I,
Vol. 2, pp. 175–205; reference on p. 184. The same letter in modernized
Spanish, with English translation, in R. H. Major, transl. and edit.:
Select Letters of Christopher Columbus, With Other Original Docu-
ments, Relating to His Four Voyages to the New World, 2nd edit.,
Hakluyt Soc. Publs., 1st Series, Vol. 43, London, 1870, pp. 183–184.

The important notes are those numbered I and VII. In neither of these is there anything to imply, or that could be construed to imply, that Columbus made his verification of a degree on the equator, measuring from east to west—a true degree of equatorial longitude. Such an operation was beyond his ability or that of anyone in his time. The imperfection of the devices for measuring time at the end of the fifteenth century was fatal to any nice calculation of longitude from eclipses. On the other hand, note VII states distinctly that the measurement was made between Lisbon and Guinea.[15]

An examination of the notes, taken together, brings out the following points which bear upon the question under discussion: (a) the Los Idolos Islands are in latitude 1° 5′ N.; (b) the starting point of the reckoning is Lisbon; (c) the navigation is from north to south; (d) a degree equals 56⅔ miles. Let it be assumed, for the moment, that Columbus was sincere in his assertion that he had actually made the verification which he asserts. It will then appear that the points just stated constitute all the facts essential to the determination of the value of a degree in accordance with the best methods pursued before the discovery of America.

[15] Nor is there anything in the notes to support the contention of Sophus Ruge (Columbus, 2nd edit., Berlin, 1902, p. 53) that Columbus claimed to have made an observation for position and then, noting the distance and sailing one degree by astronomical observation, determined the value. Cf. Vignaud, *op. cit.*, Vol. 1, p. 66, note 97.

The Method Employed by Columbus

In the first place, it should be recalled that Eratosthenes[16] had measured the length of a degree. In order to do this he had determined astronomically the latitude of two places (Syene, in Upper Egypt, and Alexandria), supposed to be on the same meridian. The distance between these two points (5000 stadia) was measured; and with these data the value of a degree was determined by a simple operation in arithmetic. The astronomers of the Caliph Al-Mamûn proceeded in an exactly similar way. They determined, by astronomical observations, the latitude of a given point. They then traveled along the meridian of that point for a measured distance. A second observation was taken; and from these data the value of 56⅔ miles for a degree was obtained.[17]

The significant matter, for this discussion, in the two cases mentioned is that the original method of measuring a degree was to determine astronomically the position of two points on the same meridian, measure the actual distance between them, and calculate the length of a degree by arithmetical computation. The contention of the present study is that Columbus followed this procedure in his verification

[16] E. H. Bunbury: A History of Ancient Geography, 2 vols., London, 1879; reference in Vol. 1, p. 621.

[17] The accounts of this famous survey are not altogether clear. Apparently several surveys were made, and the values 56, 56⅔, 57, and 57⅓ were obtained—56⅔ being the figure more commonly accepted (Géographie d'Aboulféda, Vol. 2, Part I, p. 17; Joachim Lelewel: Géographie du Moyen Âge, 4 vols., Epilogue, and atlas, Brussels, 1850–57; reference in Vol. 1, pp. xxii–xxiv.

of the length of a degree and that the erroneous information available in his day actually led him to
arrive at the old figure of 56⅔ miles.

At first sight, the opportunities open to Columbus
for determining the length of a degree may well have
seemed to promise accurate results. In the earlier
instances cited the observed points were relatively
close—in the case of Eratosthenes, the interval was
about seven degrees; in the other, much less. Of
course, the shorter the distance, the greater became
the importance of any error. For the redetermi-
nation by Columbus, on the other hand, a much
greater interval was available—approximately forty
degrees, according to the observations of the Portuguese. In fact, with the exploration of the west
coast of Africa it became possible, for the first time
in history, to carry out observations and measurements on a grand scale and over an extended interval
practically free from obstructions. Hence, it is obvious, great confidence might be placed in the results
obtained if, under the new conditions, the old value
should be arrived at.

In the new determination the two fixed points
were Lisbon and the Los Idolos Islands (or Isles de
Los; off Konakry, French Guinea). The distance
must be presumed to have been measured by re-
peated dead reckonings, as this was the regular practice of the time. All that remained for Columbus to
do, in order to verify the length of a degree, was to
make a simple arithmetical calculation. In concrete

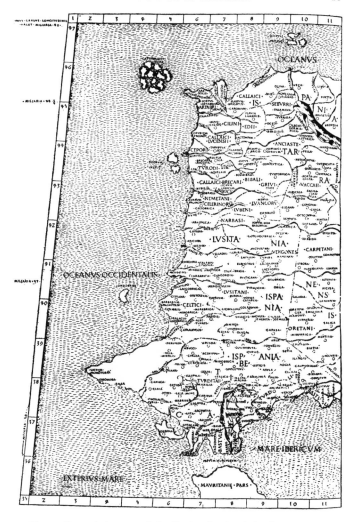

Fig. 1—Part of the map of the Iberian Peninsula in the 1490 edition of Ptolemy, to show the latitude of Lisbon (after Nordenskiöld, Facsimile-Atlas, Pl. 3).

Fig. 2—Part of gore D of Behaim's globe of
1492, with graduation transferred from gore A
to show the latitude of Lisbon (after Ravenstein, Martin Behaim, facsimile of gores of
globe).

terms: Ptolemy's map, Rome, 1490,[18] gave Oliosipo (Lisbon) as 40° 15' N. (see Fig. 1); Behaim, 1492,[19] placed it slightly above 40° N. (Fig. 2); Abulfeda,[20] in his "Geography," had placed it at 42° 40'. The Los Idolos Islands were, as we have seen (p. 6) placed at 1° 5' by Joseph. For comparison, the data may be stated in the form:

Fifteenth-Century Estimates		*Modern*[21]
Lisbon	40° 15' N	38° 42' N
Los Idolos	1° 5' N	9° 30' N
Difference	39° 10'	29° 12'

It is not known what distance in miles Columbus reckoned between these two places; I shall, therefore, take the distance as based on modern observations. If we take the accepted value of 111,121 meters for a mean meridional degree and neglect the fact that the two points are not on the same meridian,[22] we obtain a distance between the points mentioned of 3,244,769 meters. The Italian nautical

[18] A. E. Nordenskiöld: Facsimile-Atlas to the Early History of Cartography, transl. by J. A. Ekelöf and C. R. Markham, Stockholm, 1889, Pl. 3.

[19] E. G. Ravenstein: Martin Behaim: His Life and His Globe, London, 1908, with facsimile of gores of globe; reference on sheet 1, gore D.

[20] Géographie d'Aboulféda, Vol. 2, Part I, p. 244.

[21] Lisbon from "The American Ephemeris and Nautical Almanac for the Year 1925," Washington, 1923, p. 676. Los Idolos from map of the islands in 1:25,000 constituting U. S. Hydrographic Office Chart No. 2288, Washington, 1910.

[22] Lisbon is 9° 11' W. of Greenwich, Los Idolos about 13° 48' W.

mile used by Columbus contained 1480 meters.[23] We have, then, the following:

3,244,769 meters ÷ 1480 meters = 2192.4 Italian nautical miles
÷ 39⅙ (39° 10′) = 56 — Italian nautical miles to a degree

On the basis of contemporary knowledge, therefore, the method indicated in the notes of Columbus could have given no other figure than a close approximation to 56⅔ miles for the value of a degree.

CRITICISM OF CONTEMPORARY CHARTS BY COLUMBUS

In note VII, quoted above (p. 10), Columbus makes a criticism of existing charts which bears upon the point at issue. "Anyone can see," he remarks, "that there is an error in the navigation charts by measuring from north to south . . . (from) England or Ireland . . . as far as Guinea."

Now, it is a well-known fact that the portolano (navigation) charts were quite accurate for the Medi-

[23] Hermann Wagner: Die Rekonstruktion der Toscanelli-Karte vom J. 1474 und die Pseudo-Facsimilia des Behaim-Globus vom J. 1492, *Nachrichten Kön. Gesell. der Wiss. zu Göttingen: Philolog.-Hist. Klasse*, 1894, pp. 208–312; reference on p. 225 (quoted in Henry Vignaud: Toscanelli and Columbus, London, 1902, p. 200; A. E. Nordenskiöld: Periplus: An Essay on the Early History of Charts and Sailing-Directions, transl. by F. A. Bather, Stockholm, 1897, p. 23). For a critical discussion of the length of the nautical mile, see Hermann Wagner: Zur Geschichte der Seemeile, *Annal. der Hydrogr. und Marit. Meteorol.* (Hamburg), Vol. 41, 1913, pp. 393–413 and 441–450; on the Italian nautical mile see pp. 397–400.

terranean but were far from maintaining the same character for the extra-Mediterranean, or Atlantic, area.[24] An estimate of the relative error may readily be obtained by comparing the portolano charts with modern maps.

For this purpose, I have taken the distance in miles from Land's End, Cornwall, to the Strait of Gibraltar (both on the same meridian), and that from the Strait of Gibraltar to the Alexandretta corner of the Mediterranean (both nearly on the same parallel). The Mediterranean extends from longitude 5° 31′ W. to 36° 10′ E., a distance of 2333 miles, reckoning 56 statute miles to a degree on the parallel of 36°. The Strait of Gibraltar is situated in latitude 35° 57′ N.; Land's End, 50° 17′ N. approximately. The difference is 14° 20′, or 991 miles. The ratio of the distance, obtained by dividing 991 by 2333, is .425. For comparison, we may calculate the same ratio from a series of portolano charts and mappemondes:

---

[24] Nordenskiöld, Periplus, Pl. 4; Lelewel, *op. cit.*, Vol. 2, p. 33; E. L. Stevenson: Portolan Charts: Their Origin and Characteristics, *Publs. Hispanic Soc. of Amer. No. 82*, New York, 1911, pp. 19–20.

	Length of Mediterranean in inches	Land's End to Gibraltar in inches	Ratio
Catalan atlas, 1375[25]	24.17	8.75	.362
Fra Mauro, 1459[26]	12.25	4.55	.371
Genoese mappemonde, 1457[27]	7.25	2.40	.331
Catalan mappemonde, 1450[28]	9.50	3.62	.381
Jachobus Giroldis, 1426[29]	7.25	2.87	.396
Guglielmo Soleri, 1385[30]	9.00	3.06	.340
Freducci, 1497[31]	14.75	5.75	.389
Juan de la Cosa, 1500[32]	5.87	2.20	.374
Anonymous fifteenth-century portolano[33]	16.00	6.06	.378

Average   .369

If it be assumed that the scale of the Mediterranean is approximately correct in the portolano charts,

[25] J. A. C. Buchon and J. Tastu: Notice d'un atlas en langue catalane manuscrit de l'an 1375, in: Notices et extraits des manuscrits de la Bibliothèque du Roi et autres bibliothèques, Vol. 14, Part II, Paris, 1841, pp. 1–152, with an outline facsimile of the atlas in six plates; reference on Pls. 3–4. (A photographic reproduction of the atlas is given in "Choix de documents géographiques conservés à la Bibliothèque Nationale," Paris, 1883, Pls. 9–20, and also in Nordenskiöld's Periplus, Pls. 11–14.)

[26] [M. F.] Santarem: Atlas composé de mappemondes, de portulans, et de cartes hydrographiques et historiques depuis le VIe jusqu'au XVIIe siècle . . . devant servir de preuves à l'histoire de la cosmographie et de la cartographie pendant le Moyen Âge . . . , Paris, 1842–53, Pls. 43–48 (Quaritch's notation). Photographic copy was used for measurements.

[27] E. L. Stevenson: Genoese World Map, 1457. Facsimile and text, Publs. Hispanic Soc. of Amer. No. 83, New York, 1912.

[28] Konrad Kretschmer: Die katalanische Weltkarte der Biblioteca Estense zu Modena, Zeitschr. Gesell. für Erdkunde zu Berlin, Vol. 32, 1897, pp. 65–111 and 191–218; reference on Pl. 4.

[29-33] Nordenskiöld, Periplus, Pls. 4, 18, 22, 43, 19.

then the ratio, in the Atlantic area, between the distance indicated in these charts and that based on modern maps would be as .369 to .425, or .868. It follows that, if the distance, expressed in degrees, between Land's End and the Strait of Gibraltar were the same in each case, the scale of statute miles to the degree would be reduced from 69 to 59.89, or (59.89 x $\frac{1609}{1480}=$) 65.1 Italian nautical miles. However, as indicated above, the actual difference is 14° 20′, whereas the Ptolemy maps of 1490 of England and Spain[34] show a difference of 16° 23′. This would reduce the calculation in the proportion of 14° 20′ to 16° 23′, or .874, bringing the estimate of Italian nautical miles to the degree to 56.89—again a close approximation to 56⅔.

While calling attention to the fact that there was an error in the navigation charts, Columbus does not state what in his judgment the nature of this error might be. The comment which he makes (note VII, above) refers, however, to a passage in which the estimate of 56⅔ miles is attributed to Alfraganus. It is not improbable, therefore, that Columbus had reference to the difference which has just been pointed out. If so, there was no escaping the conclusion, if the Mediterranean scale was correct and if the latitudes were correct, that 56⅔ miles represented a close approximation to the length of a degree.

[34] Nordenskiöld, Facsimile-Atlas, Pl. 2: Bolerium Promõt. (Land's End), 52° 30′; Pl. 3 (our Fig. 1): northern coast of Strait of Gibraltar, 36° 7′.

THE SOURCE OF ERROR IN THE CALCULATION OF COLUMBUS

In the argument presented, there are two points which call for further comment.

As stated above, we do not know what estimate Columbus used for the distance between Lisbon and the Los Idolos Islands. My defense for introducing a modern measurement to supply this gap is that we have ample evidence in the portolano charts of the ability of fifteenth-century seamen to estimate distances by dead reckoning. The portolano charts were made by checking direction and distance.[35] It should be borne in mind that these charts were the most accurate maps produced before or during the time of Columbus. Moreover, the measurements of the portolano charts were based on the sea, not on the land[36]—a point of special significance when considered in relation to the problem before Columbus.

The second point is that the astronomical determinations of the positions dealt with are wrong. This, however, is the essential factor in the whole discussion. The error of Columbus in believing that he had verified the old estimate of 56⅔ miles to the degree springs directly from the wide inaccuracy of these determinations. Columbus himself used the best information available in his day. Why the observations should have been so far in error is not for this study to discuss; but the unquestionable fact is that

---

[35] Lelewel, *op. cit.*, Vol. 2, p. 45.

[36] *Ibid.*, pp. 47–48.

many errors did occur. As a result geographers embodying in their maps the information which came to them differed greatly in their latitudes of places.

There seem to be four well-defined stages in the evolution of the maps of Africa as regards the position in which they place the equator in relation to the coast of Upper Guinea, i.e. the coast limiting the Gulf of Guinea on the north.

Ptolemy (1490)[37] had represented the equator as crossing Africa 10 degrees south of the Canaries and indicated no such feature as the Gulf of Guinea. A relationship exists between the Ptolemy conception and that in the maps of Waldseemüller (1507),[38] Glareanus (1510),[39] Petrus Apianus (1520),[40] and the Honterus (1542).[41] The last three are derived from the Waldseemüller map, and all four represent the equator as crossing Africa about 10 degrees north of the Upper Guinea coast. The Catalan world map of 1450 also, if a legend off Cape Verde is correctly interpreted[42] to read "This cape is the end of the land. . . . This line is on the equinox . . .," represents the equator crossing well north of a gulf which may correspond to the Gulf of Guinea.

[37] Nordenskiöld, Facsimile-Atlas, Pl. 1 (our Fig. 3).

[38] Joseph Fischer and F. R. von Wieser: The Oldest Map With the Name America of the Year 1507 and the Carta Marina of the Year 1516 by M. Waldseemüller (Ilacomilus), text in English and German and facsimile of both maps, Innsbruck, 1903.

[39] Nordenskiöld, Periplus, p. 173.

[40] Nordenskiöld, Facsimile-Atlas, Pl. 38.

[41] Nordenskiöld, Periplus, p. 149.

[42] Kretschmer, Die Katalanische Weltkarte, pp. 103–104.

The concept represented by these maps seems to be the oldest one. It is followed by another, which was the concept entertained by Columbus, wherein the equator touches or comes very near to the coast of Upper Guinea. The maps of this type are the Contarini-Roselli (1506),[43] Bernardus Sylvanus (1511),[44] Ptolemy (1513),[45] Boulenger (1514),[46] Reisch (1515),[47] Laurentius Frisius (1522),[48] Ptolemy (1525),[49] Thorne (1527),[50] Bordone (1528),[51] Grynaeus (1532),[52] and Vopel (1543).[53] Three of these indicate the equator crossing the land just north of the Gulf of Guinea. The others all indicate the equator as either just grazing the coast or passing through the gulf very near the coast.

The third step in the transition from the very poor Ptolemy concept of Africa appears in one map, that known as the Hamy (1502) map,[54] which shows two equators, one marked heavily in the Indian Ocean and crossing the Gulf of Guinea region as the equator

[43] Edward Heawood: A Hitherto Unknown World Map of A.D. 1506, *Geogr. Journ.*, Vol. 62, 1923, pp. 279–293, with facsimile of map.

[44] Nordenskiöld, Facsimile-Atlas, Pl. 33.

[45] Konrad Kretschmer: Die Entdeckung Amerikas in ihrer Bedeutung für die Geschichte des Weltbildes, text and atlas, Berlin, 1892; reference in atlas, Pl. 12.

[46] *Ibid.*, Pl. 11.

[47] *Ibid.*, Pl. 10.

[48] *Ibid.*, Pl. 14.

[49] Nordenskiöld, Periplus, p. 177.

[50] Nordenskiöld, Facsimile-Atlas, Pl. 41.

[51] *Ibid.*, Pl. 39.

[52] *Ibid.*, Pl. 42.

[53] *Ibid.*, Pl. 40.

[54] Nordenskiöld, Periplus, Pl. 45.

does in the second type just described, where it is lightly marked. The other equator is marked heavily in the Atlantic and does not appear in the Indian Ocean. This second equator bears approximately the true relation to the Gulf of Guinea.

The Hamy map is only a step from the fourth type, which is approximately correct in its delineation of the relation of the equator to the Gulf of Guinea. This type is represented by the Behaim globe of 1492[55] (Fig. 2) and the La Cosa map of 1500.[56]

The series of maps have a double bearing on the Columbus project: (1) The second group furnishes indubitable evidence that the best cartographers in Europe long accepted those astronomical observations which placed the equator in substantially the same relation to Guinea as Columbus placed it. It would, therefore, appear from this evidence that there was thought to be a substantial basis for observations similar to those on which Columbus relied. (2) The maps also furnish a test of Vignaud's contention[57] that it was after his discovery of America that Columbus formulated the statement of his grand plan as that of reaching the Indies by going west. Columbus visited the Guinea country in the period when the second of the above map series was in vogue and during the period when the

[55] Ravenstein, *op. cit.*

[56] Nordenskiöld, Periplus, Pl. 43. For the primary source see below, p. 59, footnote 8.

[57] Vignaud, *op. cit.*, Vol. 2, p. 344.

third and fourth series were first appearing. It is
in the light of this last fact that Columbus' statement VI (p. 9) should be regarded: "Note that the
latitude of the climates which you will see here agrees
in all the writers; each degree corresponds to $56\frac{2}{3}$
miles. And this is a fact, and whatever anyone says
to the contrary is only words." The new observations taken about the time, or soon after the time,
that Columbus made his last voyage to Guinea were
destroying the basis of his calculation of the length
of a degree. Columbus had no faith in the new observations; this would not probably have been the
case had he been in Guinea to make them himself.
Therefore it would appear that Columbus formulated his basic concepts before he left Portugal and
not after his discovery of America.

In vindication of Columbus in thus accepting an
erroneous estimate, it should be remembered that
even an approximately correct value for the length
of a degree was not available until the determination
made by Jean Picard in 1669–1670.[58] A few years
before this date, Newton, working on the problem of
gravitation, had employed a value of approximately
60 statute miles, instead of 69+, thus underestimat-
ing the size of the earth nearly one-seventh as com-
pared with the underestimate of one-fourth by Columbus.

[58] [Louis] Vivien de Saint-Martin: Histoire de la géographie et des
découvertes géographiques depuis les temps les plus reculés jusqu'à nos
jours, text and atlas, Paris, 1873–74; reference in text, pp. 417–419.

Estimate of the Extension of Asia Eastward

We may now turn to examine the relation of the measurement of a degree to the actual undertaking of Columbus. In the quotation given above (p. 3), Vignaud says:

This fact alone [that the degree is equal to 56⅔ miles] contains in substance the entire cosmographical system which Columbus formulated later, and on which he said he had based his project. If Columbus made this observation it is necessary to recognize that we are here in the presence of a fact which may have contributed to the formation of a plan having for its object the passage by the west to the Indies.

The value of 56⅔ miles for a degree is, indeed, the key to the whole project of Columbus, for he does not appear to have used or to have had any information bearing on the extension of Asia eastward which was not commonly available to his contemporaries. The principal sources of his knowledge were Marco Polo, Sir John Mandeville, and Ptolemy.[59]

The differences of opinion discernible in the fifteenth century in regard to the position of the east coast of Asia resulted from different valuations of the length of a degree. Thus the question of the extension of Asia to the east is not a separate problem but is an integral part and, indeed, the conclusion of the discussion in regard to the length of a degree.

[59] Ravenstein, *op. cit.*, p. 71; Andrés Bernáldez: Historia de los Reyes Católicos D. Fernando y Da. Isabel, 2 vols., Seville, 1870 (also Granada, 1856), reference in Vol. I, pp. 357–358; Bartolomé de las Casas: Historia de las Indias, 5 vols., Madrid, 1875–76, reference in Book I, Chs. 5–13 (Vol. I, pp. 55–102).

A résumé of the history of the measurement of a degree is not necessary here. Suffice it to say that, among the Arabs,[60] Ptolemy's degree was reckoned at 66⅔ miles, or 22 2/9 parasangs. We have seen (p. 13) that as a result of the measurement under the Caliph Al-Mamûn it was estimated at 18 8/9 parasangs, or 56⅔ miles. From these figures there resulted varying estimates of the size of the earth. Thus, the Catalan atlas of 1375 gives the circumference as 20,052 miles;[61] the Fra Mauro map, 1459, gives it as 22,500 to 24,000 miles;[62] Columbus rated it at 20,400, according to the marginalia (notes IV, VII, VIII) quoted above. Of these estimates, that of 66⅔ miles to a degree, or 24,000 miles circumference, is the highest, and it would seem to be in comparison and in contrast with this figure that Columbus makes his reiterated statement.

According to a legend on the Bartholomew Columbus map of ca. 1503[63] (Fig. 7), Columbus and Marinus of Tyre reckoned the distance from Cape St. Vincent to Cattigara at 15 hours, or 225 degrees. Ptolemy made the same distance 12 hours, or 180 degrees. Vignaud criticizes Columbus for going

---

[60] Géographie d'Aboulféda, Vol. 1 (Introduction), pp. cclxviii ff.; Vol. 2, Part I, pp. 17–18; Lelewel, *op. cit.*, Vol. 1, pp. xxii–xxiv; Vivien de Saint-Martin, *op. cit.*, pp. 250–253.

[61] Buchon and Tastu, *op. cit.*, p. 7.

[62] Placido Zurla: Il mappamondo di Fra Mauro, Venice, 1806, p. 21.

[63] F. R. von Wieser: Die Karte des Bartolomeo Colombo über die vierte Reise des Admirals, text and facsimile of three maps, reprint from *Mitt. des Inst. für Österreichische Geschichtsforschung*, Innsbruck, 1893 (maps reproduced in Nordenskiöld, Periplus, pp. 167–169).

back to Marinus of Tyre, after Ptolemy had so conclusively demonstrated the inaccuracy of his mode of reckoning. This criticism seems to me to miss the point: Columbus did not adopt the 225 degrees of Marinus because he rejected the correction of Ptolemy. On the contrary, he made the correction of Ptolemy the basis of his own calculation. Ptolemy counted 180 degrees from the Insulae Fortunatae to the eastern edge of the known world. He bounded the Indian Sea with land on all sides. In the time of Columbus the work of the medieval travelers[64] was interpreted to have added extensively to the east of Ptolemy's known world. Behaim, in his globe of 1492[65] (Fig. 4), followed Ptolemy as far as the latter went with the map of southern Asia, placing Cattigara on the 180th meridian; but, in addition, he estimated the new East, to the eastern end of Mangi, at about 60 degrees. The total known world had thus an extent of 240 degrees from west to east. This estimate of 240 degrees, reckoned at 66⅔ miles to the degree, equaled 16,000 miles at the equator. Now, Columbus, as we have seen, accepted the value of 56⅔ miles to the degree; consequently, dividing 16,000 by 56⅔, he obtained the figure of 283 for the number of degrees in the known world. Thus he agreed with Marinus. The distance to the far East was estimated at substantially 45 degrees more than by his contemporaries. In so much he reckoned the world smaller than other people considered it.

[64] Lelewel, *op. cit.*, Vol. 2, pp. 125–126.
[65] Ravenstein, *op. cit.*, Map 2 and facsimile of globe, sheets 2, 3, and 4.

The method here employed by Columbus was exactly the same as that followed by Marinus of Tyre in reducing his itinerary distances[66] eastward to degrees and as that used by Ptolemy in correcting Marinus: the distance to the east was calculated in miles (or their equivalent), and the mileage distance was then reduced to degrees by division, employing for the degree a value determined by a measurement from north to south. Columbus thus restored to the 180 degrees of Ptolemy the 45 degrees the latter had deducted from the calculation of Marinus. In this way eastern Asia was placed at a relatively moderate distance west of Spain. One of the strange coincidences in the case is that the result obtained was a surprisingly close approximation to the position of the new lands in America.

CONCLUSION

In conclusion, the writer submits that the evidence shows Columbus to have been painstaking in his inquiries and to have utilized the best information available in his time. He was in error; but his errors, as has been shown, were of such a character as to argue convincingly for his sincerity. The fact is that a curious set of coincident inaccuracies gave Columbus every reason to believe that he had actually verified the old estimate of 56 ⅔ miles to a degree.

[66] Bunbury, *op. cit.*, Vol. 2, p. 549.

THE ROUTE OF COLUMBUS
ON HIS FIRST VOYAGE AS EVIDENCE
OF HIS KNOWLEDGE OF THE
WINDS AND CURRENTS
OF THE ATLANTIC

It has been said that there were no scientific considerations back of the voyage of 1492.[1] On the contrary the motivating cause of the expedition, in this

[1] "Rien n'indique que des considérations d'ordre scientifique aient été pour quelque chose dans l'entreprise de 1492, tandis qu'on voit clairement que pour Colomb, comme pour Pinzon et comme pour tous ceux qui s'y engagèrent, il s'agissait de la découverte d'îles et de terres nouvelles dont on espérait tirer de grands avantages, et à l'existence desquelles on croyait pour des raisons qui n'avaient rien de scientifique" (Henry Vignaud: Histoire critique de la grande entreprise de Christophe Colomb, 2 vols., Paris, 1911; reference in Vol. 2, pp. 197–198).

"Colomb avait donc des indications, cela ne peut faire l'objet d'aucun doute. Que ces indications fussent matérielles, réelles, c'est-à-dire d'ordre pratique et non dérivées de considérations théoriques, cela est également certain. Elles étaient erronées, évidemment, puisque Colomb n'a pas trouvé, où il croyait qu'elle était située, l'île ou les terres qu'il cherchait; mais elles avaient, néanmoins, un caractère de précision qui lui inspirait une confiance absolue, restée chez lui inébranlable, malgré les déceptions qu'il éprouva au cours de son exploration, et sans laquelle il n'aurait pas fait sa grande découverte" (*ibid.*, pp. 206–207).

"Remarquons bien que l'authenticité de cette histoire particulière importe peu, au fond. Ce qui est essentiel, ce qu'on doit tenir pour certain, c'est que Colomb avait des renseignements d'une nature particulière qui lui paraissaient absolument sûrs, et que c'est la confiance qu'il avait dans leur exactitude qui explique ses démarches persistantes, au milieu des circonstances les plus décourageantes, et ses exigences, autrement incompréhensibles. Que ces renseignements lui vinssent du pilote sans nom ou de toute autre manière, cela ne change rien à cette conclusion suggérée par tant de faits concordants: que le projet présenté aux Rois Catholiques et accepté par eux était basé sur des données matérielles et non sur des conceptions d'ordre spéculatif" (*ibid.*, p. 233).

view, was material information of an island or new islands hitherto unknown to Europeans. One of the facts, according to this view, tending to prove that material and not scientific reasoning actuated Columbus, was the route taken. It is contended that Columbus followed the parallel of Gomera of the Canaries[2] westwards in order to find the island of the "unknown pilot."[3] If the object of the voyage had been to reach India this route would not have been necessary. India, in the sense of being synonymous with Asia, could be reached by sailing westwards from any part of Europe.[4] Columbus did follow the paral-

[2] "Notons d'a bord que Colomb n'a pas fait voile de Palos vers l'ouest. Il s'est rendu aux Canaries, expressément pour y prendre son point de départ, et c'est de Gomera, par le 28e parallèle, qu'il a fait route vers la région occidentale où il comptait se rendre. Le choix de cette route ne s'imposait pas s'il s'agissait simplement d'aller aux Indes, et, s'il visait particulièrement les îles des Épices, il devait prendre sa direction plus au sud. On doit inférer de cela que Colomb avait un motif spécial pour choisir cette route, et cette supposition est confirmée par le fait que, tout le temps du voyage il s'attacha à suivre rigoureusement ce parallèle dont il ne consentit à s'écarter qu'avec répugnance, ainsi qu'en témoigne son Journal. On en conclut aussi qu'il croyait trouver sur cette route ce qu'il cherchait, et nous allons voir que ce n'était pas les Indes Orientales" (*ibid.*, pp. 174–175; summarized on pp. 207–209).

[3] Who on his deathbed is said to have told Columbus in Madeira of his vessel having been driven by a storm to an island far westward in the Atlantic. The main source of the story is Bartolomé de las Casas: Historia de las Indias, 5 vols., Madrid, 1875–76; reference in Book I, Ch. 14 (Vol. 1, pp. 103–106). For a general discussion of the story, with quotation of this and other sources, see Chs. 40 and 41 (Vol. 1, pp. 325–344) of J. B. Thacher: Christopher Columbus: His Life, His Work, His Remains, 3 vols., New York, 1903–04.

[4] "En même temps, il [l'auteur de la lettre dite de Toscanelli] a supprimé le passage indiquant qu'il fallait suivre le parallèle des Canaries, parceque; en fait, cette indication était inutile, car s'il s'agissait d'aller aux Indes, on pouvait prendre n'importe quel parallèle, et par conséquent elle présentait aussi le danger d'attirer l'attention sur le choix du dit

lel of the Canary Islands very closely. He only deviated from it twice during the whole voyage, once, between the dates of September 20 and 25, to search for islands and again in the final days of the voyage when the land signs in the southwest forced him to change.

This inquiry proposes to examine the matter of scientific preparation for the famous voyage of 1492. The scientific preparation has two aspects: first, a course of reasoning by which Columbus came to the conclusion that eastern Asia was not far distant west of Europe, and, second, Columbus' study of the problem of navigating the Atlantic. The first of these questions the writer has already investigated in the preceding study (pp. 27–30). This question will not be dealt with here. The second question alone will be the subject of the present study. Obviously, since it has been plausibly maintained that there was no scientific background to the voyage, it is difficult to prove directly that there was such a background. However, there are internal evidences that may properly be pointed out and examined for what they are worth.

THE ISLAND OUTPOSTS AS KEY POINTS FOR THE STUDY OF THE ATLANTIC

Columbus originated some plan of westward exploration during his stay in Portugal. Whether this plan was the same as the one he later carried out

parellèle, singulier, si le projet n'avait en vue que les Indes et n'etait fondé que sur des raisons théoriques" (Vignaud, *op. cit.*, Vol. 2, p. 559, end of footnote 7).

matters not. From Portugal he went to Spain. Hence the point of departure for his voyage brought him face to face with the same problem in navigating the Atlantic westwards as he would have had starting from Portugal. In the study of that Atlantic there were three key points whence the problem as Columbus faced it could be studied to better advantage than elsewhere. These points were the Azores, the Madeiras, and the Canaries. All three had been known to the Portuguese for many years. The reader is invited to study their position on the accompanying map (Pl. I).[5] Their position with respect to the

[5] On Pl. I the route of Columbus across the Atlantic and return has been plotted according to the day's runs and courses as given in the abstract by Las Casas of Columbus' log book (M. F. de Navarrete: Colección de los viages y descubrimientos que hicieron por mar los Españoles desde fines del siglo XV, Vol. 1, Madrid, 1825, pp. 1–166; Raccolta di documenti e studi pubblicati dalla R. Commissione Colombiana pel Quarto Centenario dalla Scoperta dell'America, Part I, Vol. 1, Rome, 1892, pp. 1–119; English translation, with occasional errors in the figures, in C. R. Markham: The Journal of Christopher Columbus During His First Voyage, 1492–93, etc., *Hakluyt Soc. Publs.*, 1st Series, Vol. 86, London, 1893, pp. 15–193). The portions between Palos and the Canaries and between the Azores and Palos have been omitted because the data for these in the log book are insufficient. The day's runs on Sept. 26, Oct. 9, and Oct. 11, which in the log book are given only as totals, have been divided into the component parts estimated by G. V. Fox in the table of distances and courses of the voyage (pp. 406–407 of The Log of Columbus Across the Atlantic Ocean, 1492, Appendix D to his: An Attempt to Solve the Problem of the First Landing Place of Columbus in the New World. Appendix No. 18 to *U. S. Coast and Geodetic Survey Rept. for 1880*, Washington, 1882, pp. 346–411). Fox's allowance of 3 leagues for departure from Gomera, Sept. 6–8, has also been used. Although a certain leeway in the interpretation of the route is possible, the necessity of fitting the outward and homeward tracks between known endpoints makes it probable that any such reconstruction will in general be correct. At all events the present reconstruction is sufficiently correct to show the relation of the route to the physical conditions of the North Atlantic.

ocean currents and the prevailing winds should especially be noted. These things were particularly important in crossing the Atlantic with sails. A proper
study of winds and currents might, under the circumstances, therefore, be denominated scientific
preparation for the great voyage, especially so if the
conduct of the voyage indicates the proper utiliza-

Of previous serious efforts to reconstruct the trans-Atlantic tracks of
the first voyage on the basis of the entries of the log book abstract four
are known to the writer: (1) the map showing the routes of the four
voyages on the equatorial scale of 1:17,500,000, in Vol. 1 of Navarrete,
work cited on p. 60, footnote 10 (copied without credit on Pl. 9 of Giuseppe Banchero's "La tavola di bronzo, il pallio di seta, ed il Codice
Colomboamericano," Genoa, 1857); (2) the map showing the westward
route of the first voyage on the equatorial scale of 1:25,000,000 on page 4
of [Oskar Peschel]: Das Schiffsbuch des Entdeckers von Amerika bei
seiner Ueberfahrt über das atlantische Meer, Das Ausland, Vol. 40, 1867,
pp. 1–11; (3) the table of daily positions in latitude and longitude of the
westward route of the first voyage adjusted to probable magnetic declination in 1492, on pp. 416–417 of C. A. Schott: An Inquiry Into the Variation of the Compass Off the Bahama Islands at the Time of the Landfall
of Columbus in 1492, Appendix No. 19 to U. S. Coast and Geodetic Survey
Rept. for 1880, Washington, 1882, pp. 412–417; (4) the map by E. G.
R[avenstein] showing the routes of the four voyages on the scale of
1:80,000,000 forming the map facing p. 1 in C. R. Markham's "Life
of Christopher Columbus," London, 1892 (copied in Filson Young's
"Christopher Columbus and the New World of His Discovery," 2 vols.,
London, 1906, and, without credit, in E. G. Bourne's "Spain in America,
1450–1580," New York, 1904). On the maps by Giuseppi Pennesi accompanying P. Amat di S. Filippo: Biografia dei viaggiatori italiani colla
bibliografia delle loro opere ("Studi Bibliografici e Biografici sulla Storia
della Geografia in Italia," published on the occasion of the Second
International Geographical Congress, Paris, 1875, by the Società Geografica Italiana, 2nd edition, Vol. 1, Rome, 1882) the route of Columbus'
first voyage (on Tavola I; equatorial scale, 1:90,000,000) is somewhat
generalized.

Although, for the purpose of tying in the route, the endpoints of the
outward and homeward voyages are known this is not strictly the case
with regard to the western endpoint of the outward voyage—the landfall
of October 12, 1492. It is the belief of the writer that the identity of
Columbus' San Salvador is not possible of definitive solution today. On

tion of such information. To base such a study on these three key points would be one indication of the mastery by Columbus of his problem.

THE WIND BELTS OF THE NORTH ATLANTIC

The passage of the Atlantic had been recognized from very early times as one dependent on the winds. Seneca said in Book I of his "Quaestiones naturales": "A ship may sail in a few days with a fair wind from the coast of Spain to that of India."[6] This is

Footnote 5, continued

the accompanying map (Pl. I) Cat Island is indicated as the landfall. The reason therefor is briefly this. It does not seem probable that the light seen by Columbus at 10 P.M., October 11 (Journal under October 11), if on land, could have been on the same island that was sighted at 2 A.M., October 12, two leagues, or 8 nautical miles away, in view of the fact that the vessels had proceeded 48 miles on their due west course in the intervening four hours. If the light was therefore on another island from the eventual landfall, Watling Island, as the one projecting farthest east from the chain, may be taken for the one on which the light was seen. Cat Island is the next to the west, and would thus best correspond to the landfall.

It should be expressly stated, however, that it is not the intention to enter into the controversy as to the identity of the landfall. The reader who wishes to pursue the question further will find references to the publications of students of the problem on pp. 350–351 of G. V. Fox's above-mentioned memoir; on pp. 52–56 of Vol. 2 of Justin Winsor: Narrative and Critical History of America, Boston, 1886; in Ch. 5 (pp. 89–107) of C. R. Markham's above-mentioned "Life of Christopher Columbus"; on pp. 9–10 of Rudolf Cronau's "The Discovery of America and the Landfall of Columbus; The Last Resting Place of Columbus: Two Monographs Based on Personal Investigations," privately printed, New York, 1921.

[6] So quoted in Ferdinand Columbus: The History of the Life and Actions of Adm. Christopher Columbus, and of His Discovery of the West Indies, Call'd the New World, Now in Possession of His Catholick Majesty, Written by His Own Son, in Awnsham Churchill and John Churchill's "A Collection of Voyages and Travels, Some Now First Printed from Original Manuscripts, Others Now First Published in

cited by Ferdinand Columbus as one of the opinions of learned men which influenced his father in the formulation of his plan and shows that he had given specific thought to this aspect of the problem. Without such favorable winds it is questionable whether any crew could have been found sufficiently courageous to have endured the voyage, given the conditions confronting the world in 1492. Now, a study of the accompanying map will show that, roughly, north of the Azores was a belt of prevailing west winds and currents making extremely unlikely the conditions laid down by Seneca. Between the Azores and the Canaries was a belt with a high percentage of calms. The winds were variable, without a prevailing east wind. But the Canary Islands mark in a general way the northern limit of the northeast trade winds. There is no obstruction to a westward voyage by the ocean currents. These winds

English" (8 vols., London, 1707–1748), Vol. 2, pp. 501–628; reference on p. 510. (The first published version is in Italian, translated from the lost Spanish original, and was printed in Venice in 1571. It is entitled: "Historie del S. D. Fernando Colombo nelle quali s'ha particolare e vera relatione della vita e de' fatti dell' ammiraglio D. Christoforo Colombo, suo padre, e dello scoprimento ch'egli fece dell' Indie occidentali, detto Mondo Nuovo, hora possedute dal S. Re Catolico, nuovamente di lingua spagnuola tradotte nell' italiana dal sig. Alfonso Ulloa.") The standard current edition of the Italian version is that edited by Giulio Antimaco and published in London in 1867.

The Latin original of Seneca reads: "Quantum enim est quod ab ultimis litoribus Hispaniae usque ad Indos iacet? Paucissimorum dierum spatium, si navem suus ferat ventus, implebit." While Seneca's main point was that the distance was short, Columbus probably regarded that as incidental, as he had his own views as to the distance, and seized rather upon the reference to the fair wind, as an important element in his plans.

vary seasonally. The conditions herein mentioned prevail farthest south in December and farthest north in July. In mid-Atlantic the northern limit of the trades varies between the 25th and 28th parallels. Near the European shore they vary from Lisbon in latitude 38° to Mogador on the Moroccan coast in 32° N.

EVIDENCES OF LAND IN THE WEST

Columbus gathered all the information he could concerning the evidences of land to the westward. Both Las Casas and Ferdinand Columbus devote considerable space to cataloguing this information.[7] But neither says anything about the problem of ocean navigation. Whatever we may learn of this phase of the problem we can only infer by calling attention to the natural phenomena in comparison with Columbus' conduct of his voyage. However, there are important consequences that may legitimately be inferred from the material catalogued by Las Casas and Ferdinand Columbus. According to them the people of the Azores had reported that once when the wind had blown many days from the west it had cast upon their shores pines of a kind which did not grow on their islands. At another time the sea brought the bodies of two men of strange race to the island of Flores, one of the Azores. Still another time covered boats, or *almadías*, had been cast upon the shore.

[7] Ferdinand Columbus, *op. cit.*, Ch. 9 (English edition, pp. 513-515); Las Casas, *op. cit.*, Book I, Ch. 13 (Vol. I, pp. 97-102).

A certain captain, Martin Vicente, told Columbus that, being 450 leagues west of Cape St. Vincent, he had picked up from the water a piece of wood curiously carved. He reported the winds had been west for many days. Pero Correa had reported to Columbus that in the island of Porto Santo of the Madeira group he had seen another piece of wood brought by the same winds. Other reports were about reeds of such a size that one joint would hold upwards of four quarts of wine. No such reeds grew in western Europe or Africa. Most of these things are mentioned in connection with the west winds. The *almadías* and the dead bodies, though, were brought by the sea. We are probably warranted in interpreting this as having reference to the currents from the west which pass the Azores. Of the stories listed above four are connected directly with the Azores and one with the island of Porto Santo, while the story of the reeds is not located. From these facts, then, it seems that it may legitimately be inferred that Columbus had his attention definitely called to the existence both of the prevailing west winds and of the easterly drift of the ocean currents in the latitude of the Azores.

As regards knowledge of the sea farther south, we have to infer from other matters. Columbus discredited the story of Antonio Leme[8] that he had seen islands west of Madeira because by his own story he had not sailed 100 leagues westward. At least if

8 Ferdinand Columbus, English edition, *op. cit.*, p. 513; Las Casas, *op. cit.*, Book 1, Ch. 13 (Vol. 1, pp. 98–99).

anything had been seen it was only rocks or mayhap
floating islands, such as the ancients had described.
From this it might be argued that Columbus was
acquainted with the Atlantic for about 300 miles
at least west of the Madeiras. According to the
deposition of Alonzo Velez Allid,[9] one Pero Vasquez
de la Frontera had talked with both Columbus and
Pinzón concerning the western sea. He told them
that "when they arrived among the grasses (*hierbas*), it would be necessary to follow a straight road
because it was impossible not to find land." This
Pero Vasquez de la Frontera, according to the testimony, was a sailor who had been on a westward voyage under the auspices of an Infant of Portugal to
find India. He said that in order to reach India it
was necessary to brave the obstacle of the grasses.
Because this had not been done the Infant of Portugal had failed to reach the Indies.[10] These grasses,
or *hierbas*, in the ocean seem to be nothing more or
less than what is called the Sargasso Sea. In that
case direct knowledge of the Atlantic was available
for over a thousand miles west of the Madeiras and
the Canaries, for the bulk of the Sargasso Sea is not
west of the Azores. It is in the belt of calms and no
ocean currents, its densest area lying between the

[9] Deposition of Alonzo Velez Allid, Nov. 1, 1532: "Que cuando llegasen
á las dichas hierbas . . . salvo que siquiesen la via derecha porque
era imposible el no dar en la tierra" (Cesáreo Fernández Duro: Colón y
Pinzón: Informe relativo á los pormenores de descubrimiento del Nuevo
Mundo presentado á la Real Academia de la Historia, Madrid, 1883,
pp. 234–235).

[10] Fernández Duro, *op. cit.*, pp. 234–235.

20th and 35th parallels of north latitude and between the 38th and 74th meridians west of Greenwich.[11] The position varies slightly with the winds and the currents.

Such is the evidence collected by Columbus before his voyage. There were rumors about the Island of the Seven Cities[12] and other mythical lands, but these need not detain us. Columbus probably had more evidence than was catalogued by his son and by Las Casas. But it has not come down to us. It should be particularly noted once more that neither Las Casas nor Ferdinand Columbus devote any space to discussing the problem of navigating the Atlantic from the seaman's standpoint. Therefore, whatever we learn on this point will be incidental to the other information they gave. It is by subjecting this information to analysis that we come into possession of the knowledge Columbus had.

The Problem of Navigating the Atlantic in the Light of Contemporary Knowledge

Now, if we imagine a present-day scientist studying the problem of navigating the Atlantic under the conditions that faced Columbus in 1492, the question arises, Just what information could he gather that would assist him in the solution of his problem? We

[11] See the map of the Sargasso Sea in W. H. Babcock: Legendary Islands of the Atlantic: A Study in Medieval Geography, *Amer. Geogr. Soc. Research Series No. 8*, New York, 1922, p. 28, and the authorities there cited on p. 30, footnote. See also Pl. I of the present work for its total area.

[12] On this topic, see Babcock, *op. cit.*, Ch. 5.

must imagine such a person confined entirely to the
eastern side of the Atlantic for all of his information.
He could make his calculation of the size of the earth.
He could inform himself as to the extent of land between the known West and the known East. From
these data he could make a calculation as to the probable distance across the Atlantic. We know that
Columbus did this. Such a scientist would also take
into account his means of travel. If confined to
sails, then he would inquire into the matter of helps
and hindrances to such travel, in other words he
would study the winds and ocean currents. He
would learn that there was a belt of prevailing westerly winds north of the Azores. Between the Azores
and the Canaries there was a belt of calms and variable winds, including a goodly percentage of head
winds unsuited to rapid progress. South from the
Canaries there was a belt of prevailing northeast and
east winds, with a low percentage of calms and very
few head winds. As for the ocean currents, there
was an easterly drift of the ocean north of the
Azores. This current turned south along the coast
of Portugal and North Africa and again moved
westward between the Canaries and the Cape Verde
Islands. Unless the inquiry were extended to the far
north and south, this would include substantially all
that our assumed present-day scientist could learn
short of crossing the ocean. If we apply this inquiry to the Columbus problem we shall see that
Columbus apparently was in possession of all of these

facts and understood them so thoroughly that he did not make a single false move in the entire voyage.

We know from the catalogue of the evidences of land in the west that Columbus knew of the prevailing west winds and the easterly drift of the Atlantic in the region of the Azores and north thereof. But we have not even a mention of the belt of calms and variable winds between the Azores and the Canaries, nor have we any mention of the prevailing northeast and east winds from the Canaries south.

Columbus' Proficiency in Navigation

We know from direct statements by Columbus that he gave very careful thought to the study of the winds and ocean currents. In a letter of 1501 he said:[13] "I went to sea very young, and have continued it to this day; and this art inclines those that follow it to be desirous to discover the secrets of this world; it is now forty years that I have been sailing to all those parts at present frequented; and I have dealt and conversed with wise people, as well clergy as laity, Latins, Greeks, Indians, and Moors, and many others of other sects; and our Lord has been favorable to this my inclination, and I have received of him the spirit of understanding. He has made me very skillful in navigation, etc." In his letter known as the Arte de Navegar letter[14] he recalls that he had advised

[13] Ferdinand Columbus, English edition, pp. 506–507; Las Casas, *op. cit.*, Book I, Ch. 3 (Vol. I, p. 47).

[14] So called where first published, in: Cartas de Indias; publícalas por primera vez el Ministerio de Fomento, Madrid, 1877, letter II. Also in Raccolta, Part I, Vol. 2, pp. 161–163, and, in facsimile, with translation, in Thacher, *op. cit.*, Vol. 3, pp. 226–241.

the King and Queen correctly in 1497 in regard to the probable day of arrival of the long-delayed Flanders fleet. This was specifically on account of his knowledge of the winds in the English Channel and in the Bay of Biscay. In his journal of his first voyage Columbus proposes "to construct a new chart for navigating on which I shall delineate all the sea and lands of the Ocean in their proper positions under their bearings."[15]   But it is needless to argue this point. Columbus was one of the foremost sailors of the world in an age of sails.

Therefore, it is sufficient to notice these things to make it apparent that every sea captain who sailed the Atlantic between the Canaries, the Azores, and the Spanish peninsula knew all the winds of that section of the Atlantic. As for Columbus' ability as a navigator, Las Casas says: "Thus we believe that Christopher Columbus in the art of navigation exceeded without any doubt all others who lived in his day."[16]

ANALYSIS OF THE WESTWARD VOYAGE

To make it still more apparent that Columbus knew the facts set forth above in regard to the Atlantic south of the Azores, the voyage outwards will

[15] Markham, Journal, p. 18. In the original, now in the Biblioteca Nacional in Madrid (Raccolta, Part I, Vol. I, p. 3), the passage reads: "tengo propósito de hazer carta nueva de navegar, en la qual situaré toda la mar & tierras del mar Ocçéano en sus proprios lugares, debaxo su viento."

[16] Las Casas, op. cit., Book I, Ch. 3 (Vol. I, p. 49): "Ansí creemos que Cristóbal Colón en el arte de navegar excedió sin alguna duda á todos cuantos en su tiempo en el mundo habia."

now be subjected to study for any internal evidences it may furnish.

The first fact that confronts one is that the voyage was made westward from the Canaries and not from Spain. It is probably true that even in 1492 the physical difficulties of the passage of the Atlantic could have been overcome anywhere between Norway and Guinea were it not for the psychological difficulties. In the first crossing the psychology of the common sailor was a matter of extreme importance. In dealing with this element it was indispensable that the passage should be accomplished in the shortest possible time. Columbus understood this perfectly. He had promised his crews that they would find land when they had gone about 750 leagues west of the island of Ferro.[17] Then from the 9th of September, the third day out of Gomera, Columbus systematically falsified the day's run as told to the crew, because, as he tells us in the Journal,[18] "if the voyage was of long duration, the people would not be so terrified and disheartened." He noted the same reason[19] again on September 25, when 21 leagues were sailed, "but the people were told that 13 was the dis-

[17] Las Casas, *op. cit.*, Book 1, Ch. 39 (Vol. 1, p. 287): "por cualquiera ocasión ó conjetura que le hobiese á su opinión venido, que, habiendo navegado de la isla del Hierro por este mar Océano 750 leguas, pocas más ó ménos, habia de hallar tierra." See also Vignaud, *op. cit.*, Vol. 2, p. 282. Reckoning at 1480 meters each (see above, p. 18, footnote 23) the four Italian nautical miles that constitute a league, this would work out to about 63° longitude west of Greenwich on the 28th parallel, or about 300 English statute miles south-southeast of Bermuda.

[18] Markham, Journal, p. 22, under date of Sunday, 9th of September.

[19] *Ibid.*, p. 29, under 25th of September.

tance made good: for it was always feigned to them
that the distances were less, so that the voyage might
not appear so long." Vignaud objects[20] to this on
two grounds: first, it was not the Admiral's but the
pilot's business to keep the log, and there were several
pilots in the fleet; second, to deceive the crew sufficiently to reach Asia he would have to falsify the log
by over 1000 leagues. This latter objection has been
considered in the preceding study (p. 27) and will
not detain us here. As for the first objection, the
pilots themselves did not agree and, according to the
Journal at least, were distinctly inferior in ability to
Columbus, as witness the Journal under dates of
September 17, February 10, and February 15.[21] Vignaud objects that this shows interpolations and pur-
poseful falsifications because Columbus could not
know the calculations of the pilots of the *Niña* and
Pinta. He overlooks the fact that conversation was
had from ship to ship on several occasions. Considering these facts it is under the aspect of reaching the
farthest west possible in the shortest space of time
possible that one should view both the choice of the
parallel of the Canaries as the one on which the voyage was made and the persistence with which Columbus stuck to that parallel.

With regard to the whole enterprise Vignaud has
said:[22] "When he left Palos with his hardy companions he was not imbued with any chimerical theory

[20] Vignaud, *op. cit.*, pp. 261–264.
[21] Markham, Journal, pp. 24, 173, and 178–179.
[22] Vignaud, *op. cit.*, Vol. 2, pp. 492–493.

about the proximity of the Indies borrowed or stolen
from a savant whose knowledge one has misunder-
stood in attributing it to him. If it had been so,
the great event which has revealed the existence of
another world would have been due to nothing but a
happy chance." Then choice, of the parallel of the
Canaries for the voyage was either a happy chance
or due to the story of the "unknown pilot." But if
the success of the voyage is due to the unknown pilot
then the happy chance is only once removed. How
shall we explain the happy chance of the pilot's return,
something the best navigators of Spain failed to accomplish for forty-five years, on the Pacific; and how
shall we explain the happy chance that enabled Columbus without error to pick the proper return route
across the Atlantic on his first voyage?

But if both of Vignaud's contentions are rejected
and in their stead we credit Columbus with a scientific study of his problem, we are not driven from one
explanation to another like the Hindu philosopher
in explaining what held the world in place. Coming
back to Columbus' westward route, inspection of the
accompanying map (Pl. I) will show that no other
route farther north could have been chosen which
would comport with either the condition of the ancients or with the necessity of making the greatest
distance in the shortest possible time. The choice
of the parallel of the Canaries comports perfectly
with the knowledge we have shown every navigator
concerned had of the Atlantic immediately west of

Spain and North Africa. It comports with the knowledge we have shown was had of the Atlantic for over a thousand miles west of the Canaries. Moreover, it is in perfect consonance with the return voyage to credit Columbus with an understanding of the problems of navigating the Atlantic. In fact, the return voyage constitutes an unanswerable argument against the contention that the discovery was all a happy chance or was based on the story of an unknown pilot.

The choice of the Canary parallel resulted in such success that after a time it brought its own troubles. The sailors began to complain that they never could get back to Spain because of the prevalence of both winds and currents from the east. On September 22 Columbus noted:[23] "This contrary wind was very necessary to me, because my people were much excited at the thought that in these seas no wind ever blew in the direction of Spain." And the next day the Admiral remarked:[24] "The high sea was very necessary to me, such as had not appeared but in the time of the Jews when they went out of Egypt and murmured against Moses, who delivered them out of captivity." In the lawsuit of Diego Columbus against the Crown, Francisco Morales, the eighth witness, answered the eighth question saying:[25] "The

[23] Markham, Journal, p. 27.

[24] Ibid., p. 28.

[25] Deposition of Francisco Morales in Porto Rico, Sept. 14, 1514: "se juntaron los maestres de tres navios que trayan el dicho primer viage, é que se pusyeron en requerir al dicho Almirante que se bolviese á Castilla, porque segund los tiempos reynavan levantes en el golfo que no creyan

captains of the three boats who were on the first voyage concerted among themselves and demanded of the Admiral that he should return to Castile, because, considering the times the east winds prevailed on the sea, they did not believe if they went any farther they would be able to return to Spain, and the said Admiral answered them that they should not concern themselves in such matters, that God who gave them these times would give to them another to return." Testimony on the same point was also given by Juan Roldan of Moguer in 1535.[26]

By the choice of the latitude of the Canaries for his route westward Columbus avoided the belt of calms and variable winds between the Azores and the Canaries. He chose a route that was well within the northern limit of the northeast trade winds at that season, as shown on the adjoining map (Pl. I). He also very nearly traveled the road marked on the same map for the present customary sailing route by way of the trades for the month of August. In other words, over four hundred years of experience in sailing the Atlantic has not suggested any material change in the route chosen by Columbus on his first

sy mas adelante yva de·poder bolver en España, y quel dicho Almirante le respondió que no curasen de aquello, que Dios que les daba aquel tienpo les daria otra para bolver" (Cesáreo Fernández Duro: De los pleitos de Colón, 2 vols., Madrid, 1892–94, in "Colección de documentos inéditos relativos al descubrimiento, conquista y organización de las antiguas posesiones españolas de ultra-mar," 2nd Series, Vols. 7 and 8, Real Academia de Historia, Madrid, reference in Vol. 7, p. 421.)

[26] Deposition of Juan Roldan of Moguer at Seville, Dec. 22, 1535 (Fernández Duro, Colón y Pinzón, p. 260).

voyage. In thirty-three days he reached land among the Bahama group of islands and so crowned the first part of his work with complete success.

THE RETURN VOYAGE

After exploring among the West Indies from October 12, 1492, to January 16, 1493, Columbus began his homeward voyage. So much has been said about his discovery of America that it has been lost to sight and thought that he also discovered both of the great sailing routes in the North Atlantic. It is in the study of this return voyage in connection with the outward voyage that the science of Columbus stands out in striking fashion. He made no attempt to return to Spain by the way he came. For the period from January 16 to February 4 he continued toward the northern latitudes (see Pl. I). In that time he made only about a third of the distance homeward across the Atlantic. But he reached a point directly west of the Azores. There he reached the latitude of the prevailing westerly winds. It was in this latitude that he really recrossed the Atlantic. In general the westerly winds are more reliable five degrees farther north. But Columbus reached a region where he did not have to contend with easterly winds. Whence came this happy inspiration? Was it another happy chance? Or was it an application of reason to the knowledge we have shown he had that in the latitude of the Azores the winds were prevailing westerlies?

CONTRAST WITH DISCOVERY OF ROUTES ACROSS THE PACIFIC

To complete this investigation it remains to contrast the passage of the Atlantic with the discovery of the routes across the Pacific. The first crossing of the Pacific from east to west was by Magellan in 1520–1521. The attempted return trip of the *Trinidad*, one of Magellan's vessels, from the Spice Islands to America in 1522 under Espinosa, did not succeed.[27] After him similarly Saavedra failed in 1528, again in 1529, Gaetan in 1543, and Ortiz de Retez in 1545.[28] The eastward passage was not accomplished until Urdaneta discovered the way in 1565.[29] There intervened between the first crossing westwards and the first eastward passage forty-five years of failure, involving also the loss of the Spice Islands to Spain.

Contrast this with the work of Columbus. On his first voyage he discovered that route which is still followed by all sailing vessels as the best possible from any part of Europe to North America. He also discovered the route homeward by way of the Azores that later experience to the present time likewise has accepted as the best. The only variation in this last is the use of the Strait of Florida and the Gulf Stream at the beginning of the route, a plan Columbus, of

[27] James Burney: A Chronological History of the Discoveries in the South Sea, or Pacific Ocean, 4 vols., London, 1803–16; reference in Vol. 1, pp. 115–118.

[28] *Ibid.*: Saavedra, pp. 151–158; Gaetan, pp. 238–239; Ortiz de Retez, pp. 241–242.

[29] *Ibid.*, pp. 269–270.

course, could not follow since he had started his return voyage from Samana Bay in the island of Haiti, ten degrees to the east of Florida.

There were really three discoveries made by Columbus instead of one. His discovery of the two ocean routes was so overshadowed by the discovery of land that it has passed unnoticed. However, in the very nature of the case the really great ocean discoveries could not be appreciated by any one until later generations had become acquainted with the whole Atlantic Ocean. By that time people forgot to give credit where it was due.

CONCLUSION

This exposition of facts connected with Columbus' first voyage does not necessarily prove him to have been a true scientist. The chain of circumstances resulting so happily may have been due entirely to chance. But it is truly extraordinary when a chain of chances fits together so perfectly. For the outward voyage there was the belt of calms and head winds to be avoided. There was the indispensable need of making a great distance westwards in a short space of time. There was the belt of favorable winds to help. But their use involved a second start from a point not obviously on the route to the place sought. There were currents and winds both adverse for the return in the region from whence Columbus started on his return voyage. There was the same belt of calms and variable winds to be avoided on the return, and, finally, by a northern detour, there was a belt of favorable winds and currents by which to make the return. Without an error, every hindrance was avoided and every assisting factor was utilized. This may be chance. But to the writer it seems that Las Casas was right, "Christopher Columbus in the art of navigation exceeded without any doubt all others who lived in his day."

DID COLUMBUS BELIEVE THAT HE REACHED ASIA ON HIS FOURTH VOYAGE?

The question to be considered here is whether Columbus did or did not think that he had reached the eastern coast of Asia on his fourth voyage. That he believed he had reached Asia has been maintained by John Fiske, A. E. Nordenskiöld, and Henry Vignaud.[1] Justin Winsor, Henry Harrisse,

[1] John Fiske: The Discovery of America, With Some Account of Ancient America and the Spanish Conquest, 2 vols., Boston, 1892; reference in Vol. 1, p. 510.

A. E. Nordenskiöld: Periplus: An Essay on the Early History of Charts and Sailing-Directions, transl. by F. A. Bather, Stockholm, 1897. p. 100.

Henry Vignaud: Toscanelli and Columbus, London, 1902, pp. 215–216. Vignaud is not so positive in his "Histoire critique de la grande entreprise de Christophe Colomb," 2 vols., Paris, 1911 (see Vol. 1, p. 3, and Vol. 2, pp. 364, 455, 484, and 494), as in his earlier work. While he still credits Columbus with the belief that he had reached the confines of Asia, he quotes a long list of contemporary writers (Vol. 2, pp. 287–317) and cartographers (pp. 317–321) to show that Columbus stood almost alone in this opinion.

Other writers who take this view are:

Washington Irving: The Life and Voyages of Christopher Columbus, 3 vols., New York, 1828, Book 7, Ch. 4.

W. H. Prescott: History of the Reign of Ferdinand and Isabella the Catholic, 3 vols., Boston, 1838, Part II, Ch. 9. See also his "History of the Conquest of Mexico," 3 vols., New York, 1843, Book 2, Ch. 1.

Sir Arthur Helps: The Spanish Conquest in America, 4 vols., London, 1856–61 (Vol. 1, p. 95); new edit., edited by M. Oppenheim, 4 vols., London, 1900–04 (Vol. 1, p. 57).

J. G. Kohl: A History of the Discovery of the East Coast of North America, Particularly the Coast of Maine, from the Northmen in 990 to the Charter of Gilbert in 1578, constituting Vol. 1 of the "Docu-

BELIEF IN ASIA 55

and John Boyd Thacher are of the opposite opinion.[2] In general, it may be said that, before 1892, it was not doubted that Columbus died in the conviction

mentary History of the State of Maine" (Collections of the Maine Historical Society, 2nd Series), Portland, 1869, pp. 149 and 238–239. See also his "Asia and America," *Proc. Amer. Antiquarian Soc.*, Worcester, Mass., Vol. 21 (N. S.), 1911, pp. 284–338; reference on p. 290.

Henry Stevens: Historical and Geographical Notes on the Earliest Discoveries in America, 1453–1530, New Haven, 1869, p. 33.

H. H. Bancroft: Central America (History of the Pacific States of North America, Vols. 1–3), 3 vols., San Francisco, 1882–87; reference in Vol. 1, p. 233.

Francesco Tarducci: The Life of Christopher Columbus, transl. by H. F. Brownson, 2 vols. in one, Detroit, 1891; reference in Vol. 2, pp. 219–220.

C. K. Adams: Christopher Columbus, His Life and His Work, London, 1892, p. 255.

Edward Channing: A History of the United States (5 vols. published, 1905–21), Vol. 1, p. 18.

J. E. Olson and E. G. Bourne, edits.: The Northmen, Columbus and Cabot, 985–1503 (Original Narratives of Early American History), New York, 1906; reference in section "Original Narratives of the Voyages of Columbus," edited by E. G. Bourne, p. 397.

H. P. Biggar: The New Columbus, *Ann. Rept. Amer. Hist. Assoc. for the Year 1912*, Washington, 1914, pp. 95–104; reference on p. 104.

C. R. Beazley: The Columbian Tradition on the Discovery of America, [by] Henry Vignaud (a review), *Geogr. Journ.*, Vol. 56, 1920, pp. 416–418.

[2] Justin Winsor: Christopher Columbus, and How He Received and Imparted the Spirit of Discovery, Boston, 1891, pp. 296 and 437–476. See also his "Cartier to Frontenac," Boston, 1894, pp. 1–4.

Henry Harrisse: The Discovery of North America: A Critical, Documentary, and Historic Investigation, London and Paris, 1892, p. 104.

J. B. Thacher: Christopher Columbus: His Life, His Work, His Remains, As Revealed by Original Printed and Manuscript Records, 3 vols., New York, 1903–04; reference in Vol. 2, pp. 568 and 617.

Other writers who think Columbus believed that he had discovered a new world are:

A. J. Weise: The Discoveries of America to the Year 1525, New York, 1884, p. 154.

C. R. Markham: Life of Christopher Columbus, London, 1892, p. 283.

that he had reached Asia. Since then, however, many scholars have adopted the view that it had dawned upon Columbus, before his death, that he had discovered a new world distinct from the India and Cathay which had been the original object of his search.

The present discussion upholds the earlier conclusion and examines in detail the arguments advanced against it by Harrisse and Thacher, taken as representative of the later view.

THE BASIS FOR A NEW INVESTIGATION

Columbian scholars have devoted themselves almost exclusively to a study of the documentary materials on Columbus. Little attention has been given to the cartographical evidence, aside from the reconstructions of the so-called Toscanelli chart. But in the writings of Columbus there are so many references to his geographical beliefs that a study based on cartography may assist in determining whether Columbus did or did not believe that he had reached eastern Asia while on the coast of Veragua (Panama).

Footnote 2, continued

Filson Young: Christopher Columbus and the New World of His Discovery, 2 vols., Philadelphia, 1906; reference in Vol. 2, pp. 164 and 169.

E. L. Stevenson: Marine World Chart of Nicolo de Canerio Januensis, 1502 (circa): A Critical Study, With Facsimile (text, 1908; facsimile in portfolio, 1907), Amer. Geogr. Soc. and Hispanic Soc. of America, New York; reference in text, pp. 29-30.

As we have seen in the first study (p. 6), Columbus had read (we still have preserved in the Biblioteca Colombina at Seville his annotated copies) the "Imago mundi" of Pierre d'Ailly, the "Historia rerum ubique gestarum" of Aeneas Sylvius, and the first Latin edition of Marco Polo's travels, entitled "De consuetudinibus et condicionibus orientalium regionum."[3] He had also read the "Travels of Sir John Mandeville"[4] and the "Geography" of Ptolemy.[5] Moreover, we have to assist us in a study of Colum-

[3] Justin Winsor, edit.: Narrative and Critical History of America, 8 vols., Boston, 1884–89; reference in Vol. 2, pp. 26–33.

Vignaud, Histoire critique, Vol. 1, pp. 95–104.

Postille. In: Raccolta di documenti e studi pubblicati dalla R. Commissione Colombiana pel Quarto Centenario dalla Scoperta dell'America, 6 parts in 14 vols., Rome, 1892–96; reference in Part I, Vol. 2, pp. 291–470.

Biblioteca Colombina: Catálogo de sus libros impresos, Seville, 1888–1916, Vol. 1, pp. 49–69; Vol. 2, pp. vii–xliv; Vol. 5, p. 51.

[4] First published in French between 1357 and 1371. See J. O. Halliwell, edit.: The Voiage and Travaile of Sir John Maundeville, Kt. . . . Reprinted from the Edition of A. D. 1725, London, 1839.

[5] The "Geography" ("Geographiké hyphégesis") of the Greek geographer Claudius Ptolemaeus of Alexandria (ca. 150 A.D.), which exerted so profound an influence on the geographical thought of the later Middle Ages, was probably first printed, in Latin, in Vicenza in 1475. The first printed edition to be accompanied by maps was that published in Rome in 1478. Columbus possessed a copy of this edition (Raccolta, Part I, Vol. 2, p. 523). Although the work as originally written by Ptolemy was probably accompanied by maps, the maps in the printed edition are presumably independent compilations by medieval commentators from the specific data as to geographical positions given in the text. The first of these maps, reproduced in Fig. 3, is the most important as it shows Ptolemy's conception of the then known world.— The standard critical editions of the text are those by C. F. A. Nobbe, 3 vols., Leipzig, 1843–45, new edition 1888–1913, and by Charles Müller (only Books I–V of a total of eight), with Latin translation, 2 vols. and atlas, Paris, 1883 and 1901.

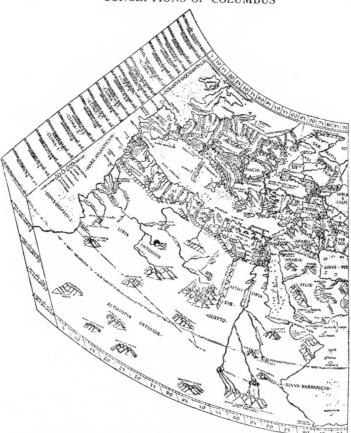

Fig. 3—Ptolemy's map of the known world in 150 A.D. from the printed

bian geography the three Bartholomew Columbus
sketch maps (ca. 1503) found by Wieser in Florence,[6]

[6] F. R. von Wieser: Die Karte des Bartolomeo Colombo über die
vierte Reise des Admirals, text and facsimile of three maps, reprint from
Mitt. des Inst. für Österreichische Geschichtsforschung, Innsbruck, 1893
(maps reproduced in Nordenskiöld, Periplus, pp. 167–169).

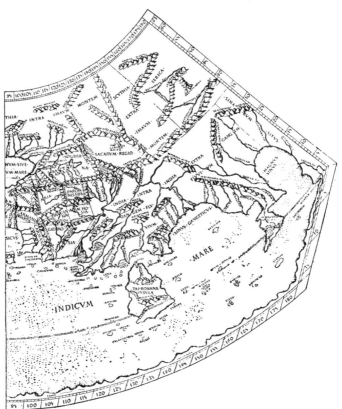

edition of 1490 (after the facsimile in Nordenskiöld, Facsimile-Atlas, Pl. 1).

(Figs. 5–7), to which may be added the Behaim globe[7] (Fig. 4) and the map of Juan de la Cosa[8] (Fig. 10

[7] E. G. Ravenstein: Martin Behaim, His Life and His Globe, London, 1908, with facsimile of the gores of the globe.

[8] Antonio Vascáno: Ensayo biográfico del célebre navegante y consumado cosmógrafo Juan de la Cosa y descripción é historia de su famosa

see also Pl. II). With these materials we may proceed to reconstruct the Columbian geography of 1502.

THE GEOGRAPHICAL BACKGROUND

We are not as much concerned with the southern coast of Asia (beyond the question of its extent east and west) as we are with the eastern coast. Ptolemy[9] made the distance from the Fortunate Isles (Canary Islands), his prime meridian on the west, to Cattigara on the east, 180° (Fig. 3 and Pl. II). Ptolemy also recorded the ideas of Marinus of Tyre, who made the same distance equal 225° instead of 180°. Columbus accepted the views of Marinus in preference to those of Ptolemy. When, on his fourth voyage, he had learned from the natives of Veragua of the gold mines of Ciguare and of the sea beyond, he wrote:[10]

Footnote 8, continued

carta geográfica, Madrid, 1892, text in Spanish, French, and English, accompanied by a facsimile of the map in the original colors edited by Cánovas Vallejo and Traynor. There are reproductions in black and white in [E. F.] Jomard: Les monuments de la géographie, ou recueil d'anciennes cartes européennes et orientales . . . Paris [1842–62], Pls. XVI, 1, 2, 3; and Nordenskiöld, Periplus, Pls. 43–44.

[9] A. E. Nordenskiöld: Facsimile-Atlas to the Early History of Cartography, transl. by J. A. Ekelöf and C. R. Markham, Stockholm, 1889, Pl. 1 (our Fig. 3) and p. 4.

[10] Letter of July 7, 1503, on the fourth voyage. In Raccolta, Part I, Vol. 2, pp. 175–205; reference on pp. 183–184. The version on pp. 296–312 of M. F. de Navarrete: Relaciones, cartas y otros documentos concernientes á los cuatro viages que hizo el Almirante D. Cristóbal Colón para el descubrimiento de las Indias occidentales (forming Vol. 1 of his "Colección de los viages y descubrimientos que hicieron por mar los Españoles desde fines del siglo XV, 5 vols., Madrid, 1825–37), in mod-

Tanbién esto que io supe por palabra, avíalo io sabido largo por escrito. Ptolomeo creió de aver bien remedado á Marino, i ahora se falla su escritura bien propinqua al cierto. Ptolomeo assienta Catigara á doçe líneas lejos de su ocçidente, que él assentó sobre el cabo de S. Vicente, en Portugal, dos grados i un terçio. Marino en .15. líneas constituió la tierra, é términos. . . . El mundo es poco; el injuto d'ello es seis partes, la séptima sólamente cubierta de agua. La experiençia ia está vista, i la escriví por otras letras, i con adornamiento de la Sacra Escritura . . . (What I learned from the mouth of these people I already knew in detail from books. Ptolemy thought that he had satisfactorily corrected Marinus, and yet this latter appears to have come very near the truth. Ptolemy places Catigara at a distance of twelve lines [hours] from his western meridian, which he fixes at two degrees and a third beyond Cape St. Vincent in Portugal. Marinus comprises the earth and its limits in fifteen lines [hours].[11] . . . The world is but small; out of seven divisions of it the dry part occupies six, and the seventh only is covered by water. Experience has shown it, and I have written it with quotations from the Holy Scripture, in other letters. . . .)

Since Columbus was seeking India, on the southern coast of Asia, as well as Cathay, on the eastern

ernized Spanish, with English translation, is reproduced in R. H. Major, transl. and edit.: Select Letters of Christopher Columbus, With Other Original Documents, Relating to His Four Voyages to the New World, 2nd edit., *Hakluyt Soc. Publs.*, 1st Series, Vol. 43, London, 1870, pp. 175–211; reference on pp. 183–184.

[11] Cf. the legend between Africa and South America on one of the Bartholomew Columbus maps (Fig. 7): "Secõdo Marino e Col° da C. Sã Vicẽtio a Cathicara g. 225, sõ hore 15. Secõdo Ptol. infine a Cattigara g. 180 che sia hore 12."

coast, the Ganges River, India intra Gangem, India extra Gangem, the Magnus Sinus, Taprobana Insula, the Aurea Chersonesus, the Indicum Mare, and Cattigara are places of importance (Fig. 3 and Pl. II). With this our concern for southern Asia stops.

Ptolemy did not interpret his information concerning Asia in such a way as to allow for an eastern coast within the limits of the known world.[12] Instead, he understood that the coast line turned southwards to form a Magnus Sinus (China Sea). The eastern coast of the Magnus Sinus with the Terra Incognita joined the African coast, making a landlocked sea of the Indicum Mare (Fig. 3).

In the Middle Ages additional information brought back by traders and travelers gave positive knowledge of the eastern coast of Asia. Of a number of these travelers Marco Polo is the best known; and from his account several prominent features of the eastern Asiatic coast were derived.[13]   These are reflected in the representation of this region on the Behaim globe[14] (Fig. 4). Cipangu was a great island situated 1500 miles eastward from Mangi. What we call China was divided into two parts: the northern, called Cathay; the southern, Mangi. Mangi

---

[12] G. E. Gerini: Researches on Ptolemy's Geography of Eastern Asia (Further India and Indo-Malay Archipelago), *Asiatic Society Monographs No. 1*, London, 1909, pp. 25, 302–304, and map at end of volume.

[13] Sir Henry Yule, trans. and edit.: The Book of Ser Marco Polo the Venetian Concerning the Kingdoms and Marvels of the East, 3rd edit., revised . . . by Henri Cordier, 2 vols., London, 1903; reference in Vol. 2, pp. 253–298.

[14] Ravenstein, *op. cit.*, Map 2.

faced south upon a great indentation of the sea, called the Sea of Chin. In this sea were a vast number of islands (estimated at 7459), mostly inhabited. The Sea of Chin bounded Mangi on the south for 1500 miles. The coast ended somewhat south of west, and two months were required to

Fig. 4—The eastern hemisphere on Behaim's globe of 1492 (after the reduction to map form in Ravenstein, Martin Behaim, Map 2).

The geographical features in bold outline with names in heavy lettering were derived from Ptolemy; those in broken outline with underscored names, from Marco Polo; the remainder from other sources.

navigate it. From western Mangi the shore turned south. The country on the west of the Sea of Chin was called Ciamba. Much gold dust was found on the coasts of the Sea of Chin. South and southeast from Ciamba, at a distance of 1500 miles, was Java, reputed to be the largest island in the world. Twelve hundred miles south and southwest of Ciamba was Lochac (or Loach), a part of the mainland. To the south of Lochac were two great islands, named Pentan and Java Minor. Java Minor was so far south that the North Star was not visible.

Besides the Behaim globe several maps embodying these features were constructed in the time of Columbus: of these the mappemonde of Henricus Martellus Germanus,[15] the already mentioned Bartholomew Columbus maps[16] (Figs. 5–7), and the Waldseemüller (1507) map[17] may be taken as examples. The Bartholomew Columbus maps attempt, of course, to harmonize the new discoveries with previous knowledge; the others either do not contain the new discoveries or, like Waldseemüller, apparently separate them from Asia.

---

[15] Of uncertain date, about 1489 according to Ravenstein, *op. cit.*, pp. 66–67. Reproduced in Nordenskiöld, Periplus, p. 123.

[16] See, above, footnote 6.

[17] Joseph Fischer and F. R. von Wieser: The Oldest Map with the Name America of the Year 1507 and the Carta Marina of the Year 1516 by M. Waldseemüller (Ilacomilus), text in English and German and facsimile of both maps, Innsbruck, 1903.

Map to Illustrate These Geographical Ideas

We may now attempt to construct a map embodying the ideas that were familiar to Columbus. The accompanying map (Pl. II) is based upon a comparison of Ptolemy, Behaim's globe, the Bartholomew Columbus maps, and the writings of Columbus. The configuration of Ptolemy (Fig. 3) is used for the southern coast of Asia, stretched in longitude, however, to conform to Marinus of Tyre, with whose views as to the eastward extension of Asia Columbus agreed, as we have seen (p. 29). This stretching is only necessary east of the crossing of the Euphrates at Hieropolis, 72° east of Ptolemy's prime meridian (Fig. 3; beyond the border of Pl. II), as west of this point Ptolemy accepted the longitudes of Marinus of Tyre.[18] Longitudes east of the Euphrates are obtained by subtracting 72° from the Ptolemaic longitude to obtain a base, then multiplying the remainder by 17/12 so as to place Cattigara 225° east of the prime meridian (Marinus' conception) instead of 180° (Ptolemy's conception).[19] (To convert these longitudes to longitudes from Greenwich, 17⅔° should be subtracted, this being the difference between Greenwich and the conventional meridian of Ferro, the

[18] Vignaud, Histoire critique, Vol. 1, p. 256; Nordenskiöld, Facsimile-Atlas, p. 4.

[19] 17/12 = ratio of 225−72 to 180−72.

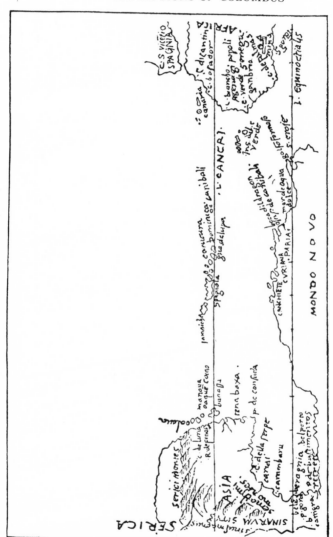

Figs. 5–7—Three sketch maps drawn by Bartholomew Columbus on the margin of a copy of a letter written by his brother Christopher in Jamaica on July 7, 1503, which illustrate Columbus' geographical conceptions during his fourth voyage (after the facsimile in von Wieser, Die Karte des Bartolomeo Colombo, Pls. 1–3).

Fig. 5—The North Atlantic area.

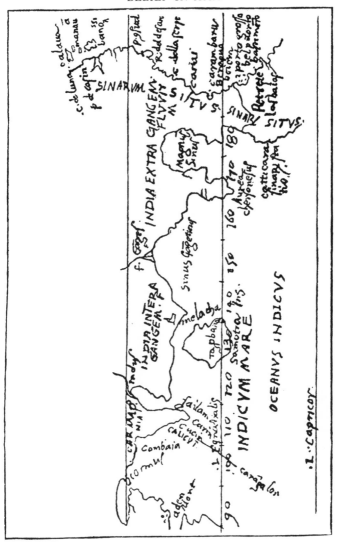

Fig. 6—Asia

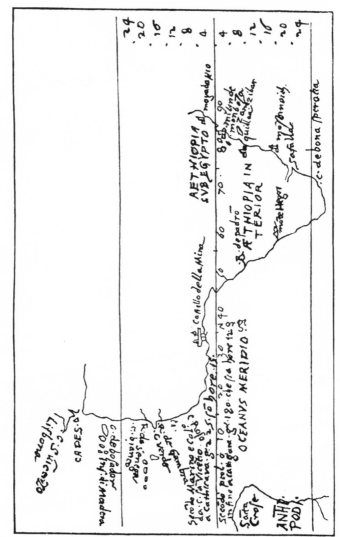

Fig. 7—Africa

equivalent of Ptolemy's prime meridian in the Fortunate Isles.) At Cattigara as the coincident point ("Cael" on the Behaim globe) there is then added to the Ptolemy configuration the coast line of eastern Asia according to the Behaim globe.[20]

Two other land positions are shown on the map. One is the eastern coast of Asia transposed so as to bring the cape at Zaitun on the same meridian as the eastern end of Cuba. This illustrates Columbus' idea of the position of the continental shore as it confronted him on his fourth voyage, inasmuch as from his first and second voyages he took Cuba to be the mainland of Asia, its eastern end corresponding to the cape at Zaitun.

The other is the coastal outline of America from the Juan de la Cosa world map of 1500,[21] which incorporates Columbus' discoveries to that date, superimposed in such a manner that the position of the Strait of Gibraltar on the Cosa map is made to coincide with its true position on the modern map. The coast is drawn in the same relative position according to latitude and longitude as on the Cosa map, the equator and Tropic of Cancer on that map affording an evaluation of the length of degree used in its rectangular projection. The resulting image brings Española, as located from Columbus' own voyages, close to Cipangu and illustrates how plausible it was for him to take the one for the other.

---

[20] Ravenstein, *op. cit.*, Map 2.
[21] See, above, footnote 8 and, below, Fig. 10.

IDENTIFICATIONS MADE BY COLUMBUS

It was on his first voyage that Columbus identified Española as Cipangu; he confused the name Civao, a local Indian name, with Cipangu. Cuba he took to be a part of Mangi: its northern shore trended in the direction indicated by Behaim and Martellus. The southern coast of Cuba seemed to him to correspond with the southern coast of Mangi. He had coasted Cuba for a great distance—335 leagues on his second voyage—until he became convinced that Cuba was the mainland. An oath affirming this belief was administered to the crew;[22] after which Columbus turned back to Española. The puzzling thing about Cuba was the fact that it did not seem to contain the great cities he looked for, and that it was so close to Española, or Cipangu. On the third voyage Columbus had gone farther south and touched the coast of South America near the mouth of the Orinoco River. Here, again, he found partial confirmation of his geographical beliefs. The land found was almost exactly in the position of islands indicated by Behaim, modified by the addition of the 45° to Ptolemy. The 7459 islands were there and were inhabited by savages, as both Marco Polo and Mandeville had said. The disturbing factor this time was the evidently continental proportions of the land.

[22] Quoted with translation (after Navarrete, pp. 143–149 of Colección de documentos concernientes á la persona, viages y descubrimientos del Almirante D. Cristóbal Colón, forming Vol. 2 of the work cited in footnote 10) in Thacher, *op. cit.*, Vol. 2, pp. 322–332.

Of course, on his first voyage Columbus had not seen the Behaim globe and probably not the Martellus mappemonde. But maps are rarely the original compositions of map makers; they are made from earlier maps and other data. Behaim and Columbus drew their geographical ideas from the same source. The map constructed by Ravenstein to show Behaim's use of Marco Polo (Fig. 4) will go far to justify a presumption that Columbus had similar ideas. The hypothesis may be adopted; it will be justified if the movements and writings of Columbus harmonize with the hypothesis. This study endeavors to show that his actions and his writings cannot be made to harmonize with any other cartographical hypothesis so far advanced.

MOVEMENTS OF COLUMBUS AS REFLECTION OF HIS VIEWS

It has been contended that, if Columbus really believed himself to be on the coast of Asia on his fourth voyage, he would have directed his efforts to following the new lands either north or south to the regions so well known in theory to all cosmographers.[23] That is exactly what he tried to do. He had a choice of turning either north or south, and he himself gives his reason for not turning north. Let us briefly reconsider his experience.

On his first voyage he had turned south, when on the northeast coast of Cuba, because it was winter

---

[23] Harrisse, *op. cit.*, p. 105.

and he did not wish to enter northern latitudes at that season.[24] On this second voyage he had explored the southern coast of Cuba with the idea, according to his friend Andrés Bernáldez, curate of the village of Los Palacios near Seville, of returning to Europe around the southern coast of Asia and either by the south of Africa or by the Red Sea and the Mediterranean.[25]

On his fourth voyage he was completing the work begun on the second. It being late in July, 1502, when he reached the southern coast of Cuba, he expected the voyage to last over into the winter season; and indeed it was the following late summer before it was completed. Under these circumstances, he turned southwest for the India of the Ganges. In so doing he was sailing from one point on the coast of Asia to another point on the same coast by a short cut, as is apparent from the map (Pl. II). Pedro de Ledesma, the chief pilot, testified under oath before the fiscal that Columbus ran southwest in search of Asia.[26] When the fleet sighted the coast of Honduras it was recognized as the coast of Ciamba.

---

[24] Letter to Luis de Santangel dated Feb. 15, 1493, with postscript of March 14, 1493, in Raccolta, Part I, Vol. 1, pp. 120–135, reference on p. 121; also in Major, Select Letters, 2nd edit., pp. 1–18, reference on p. 3.

[25] Andrés Bernáldez: Historia de los Reyes Católicos D. Fernando y Da. Isabel, 2 vols., Granada, 1856 (also Seville, 1870), Ch. 123, as cited by Irving, op. cit., Book 7, Ch. 4, on the basis of the then still unpublished work.

[26] Deposition of Pedro de Ledesma, Seville, Feb. 12, 1513: "é de alli corrieron en sur sudueste en busca del Asya, que es en la tierra firme" (Cesáreo Fernández Duro: De los pleitos de Colón, 2 vols., Madrid,

The plan was to follow this coast in a southerly and ultimately westerly direction past Java Major, Pentan, Seilan, the Strait of Malacca, and into the Indian Ocean to the India of the Ganges.

When the coast was found to run east and west nothing was more natural, on such an hypothesis, than for Columbus to turn eastwards. He was by theory on the eastern shore of Asia: to go south he should keep the shore on his right; to keep it on his left would lead him back around the coast of Ciamba and Mangi to Española. Unless Columbus was guided almost entirely by such a theory he would certainly have expected to find his strait north instead of south from Honduras, because he had encountered strong northwestward currents as he crossed the sea from Cuba to Honduras. But he persisted in his course to the south, rounded Cape Gracias á Dios, and proceeded down the coast of Honduras, Nicaragua, and Costa Rica. The eastward trend of the coast did not worry him because Marco Polo had described the course from Ciamba as between south and southeast to Java.[27] Moreover, the country was full of gold, as Polo had described the lands bordering the Sea of Chin. If further confirmation were needed, the natives told

1892–94, in "Colección de documentos inéditos relativos al descubrimiento, conquista y organización de las antiguas posesiones españolas de ultramar," 2nd series, Vols. 7 and 8, Real Academia de Historia, Madrid; reference in Vol. 7, p. 263).

27 Marco Polo, Book 3, Ch. 6 (Yule, *op. cit.*, Vol. 2, pp. 272–275).

him of the sea on the other side of Veragua at nine days' journey,[28] which fitted in with his theory that he was then on the eastern side of the Lochac, or Loach, peninsula.

Notice again the situation: Columbus was on the Caribbean coast of Central America (the land was called Veragua); he had come from Española (or Cipangu); past Cuba (or Mangi); down the coast of Central America (or Ciamba). By continuing south he would pass between Asia and the continental land discovered on his third voyage, in 1498. Ciamba was on a peninsula surrounded on three sides by the sea. On the other side the land was called Ciguare: Ciguare had "the same bearings with respect to Veragua, as Tortosa has to Fontarabia, or Pisa to Venice,"[29] i.e. they were on opposite sides of a peninsula. Columbus also understood the Indians to tell him that, on the other side, the people wore clothes; they had ships which carried guns; they had fairs and markets; they knew the pepper plant; and had horses which they used in battle. At ten days' distance from Ciguare, they also said, was the country of the Ganges River. The land of Ciguare, the Aurea Chersonesus, and the Ganges country were therefore, in the mind of Columbus, all neighboring. Columbus contended that the mines of the Aurea Chersonesus, where, according to Josephus,

[28] Letter of July 7, 1503, in Raccolta, Part I, Vol. 2, p. 183; also, with English translation, in Major, *op. cit.*, p. 181.

[29] Major, *op. cit.*, p. 182 (Raccolta, Part I, Vol. 2, p. 183).

Solomon obtained his gold, were the identical mines of Veragua.

At this point it is of interest to notice the similarity of the statements of Columbus and of Behaim relating to these mines. Columbus said:[30]

There were brought to Solomon at one journey six hundred and sixty-six quintals of gold, besides what the merchants and sailors brought, and that which was paid in Arabia. Of this gold he made two hundred lances and three hundred shields, and the entablature which was above them was also of gold and ornamented with precious stones: many other things he made likewise of gold, and a great number of vessels of great size, which he enriched with precious stones. This is related by Josephus in his Chronicle "de Antiquitatibus"; mention is also made of it in the Chronicles and in the Book of Kings. Josephus thinks that this gold was found in the Aurea; if it were so, I contend that these mines of the Aurea are identical with those of Veragua.

Behaim placed a legend on his globe just below the mouth of the Ganges which read:[31]

In the Book of Genesis it is stated that this country through which flows the Ganges is called Havilla. The best gold in the world is said to grow there. In Holy Writ, in the 3rd Book of Kings, chapters 9 and 10, it is written that King Solomon sent his ships hither and had brought from Ophir to Jerusalem of this gold and valuable pearls and precious stones. This country of Gülat

30 Major, *op. cit.*, pp. 203–204 (Raccolta, Part I, Vol. 2, p. 201).

31 Ravenstein, *op. cit.*, p. 94.

and Ophir, through which flows the river Ganges or the water of Gion, belonged together.

With this belief, why did Columbus not go on and reach the Ganges country? He tells us why.[32] "With one month of fair weather I shall complete my voyage. As I was deficient in ships, I did not persist in delaying my course." He returned to Española because his boats were in such condition that he simply could go no farther. The voyage was pressed to the extreme limit of endurance. In fact, two of his vessels had to be abandoned on the coast of Veragua. The other two had to be beached in Jamaica before reaching Española.

The principal discrepancy between what Columbus found and what he expected to find was the absence of the great cities and the great trading fleets. On this score he writes[33] that the absence of horses with saddles and poitrels and bridles of gold "is not to be wondered at, for the lands on the sea-coast are only inhabited by fishermen, and moreover I made no stay there, because I was in haste to proceed on my voyage."

Hitherto the question as to whether Columbus did or did not believe that he had reached the coast of

[32] Major, *op. cit.*, p. 206 (Raccolta, Part I, Vol. 2, p. 202). Cf. also Major, p. 193 (Raccolta, Part I, Vol. 2, p. 194).

[33] Major, *op. cit.*, p. 199 (Raccolta, Part I, Vol. 2, p. 198). On the Catalan atlas of 1375 (fascimile in "Choix de documents géographiques conservés à la Bibliothèque Nationale," Paris, 1883, Pls. 9–20; also in Nordenskiöld's "Periplus," Pls. 11–14) the southeastern coast of Asia is depicted with naked fishermen in the sea.

Asia has been argued, almost exclusively, from the standpoint of whether he was right or wrong. Since he was very far wrong, it is an easy step to the inference that he knew he was not on the coast of Asia. The question should not, however, be approached in this way. We should endeavor to put ourselves in the position of Columbus and ask whether it were possible for another person to reach his conclusion. As is well known, many people in his time maintained that the land discovered by Columbus was not Asia; there was a conflict of two schools of geography: the Marinus of Tyre-Columbian (as we might call one of them) and the Ptolemaic. In view of the vague knowledge of the East, the uncertainty as to the size of the earth, and the surprising parallel of what Columbus had found in the West Indies with what was then believed of the East, there seems little reason to doubt that anyone in the position of Columbus might well have believed or persuaded himself that he had reached Asia. Columbus never discovered his error; or, possibly, we should say that it was never proved to him that he was in error.

THE VESPUCIUS VOYAGE OF 1497

Incidentally, this discussion of the fourth voyage tends to throw some light on the disputed voyage of Vespucius of 1497. Fiske[34] and Varnhagen[35] believe

[34] Fiske, *op. cit.*, Vol. 2, pp. 53–54.

[35] F. A. de Varnhagen: Amerígo Vespucci: Son caractère, ses écrits (même les moins authentiques), sa vie et ses navigations. Lima, 1865;

the voyage to have been made and the route to have led through the Strait of Yucatan, around the Gulf of Mexico, and out by the Strait of Florida. But granted the probability of the voyage, this route does not seem likely. Columbus could not have retained his theories of Asiatic geography if his friend Vespucius or anyone else, before 1502, had proved Cuba to be an island. It is decidedly improbable that if a friend like Vespucius had made a voyage through the Straits of Yucatan and Florida in 1497 Columbus would not have known about it in 1502. It is true that Juan de la Cosa depicts Cuba as an island in 1500 (Pl. II and Figs. 10 and 11); but that is only a theoretical delineation. Such a striking feature as the Florida peninsula could hardly have escaped notice if the coast lines had been drawn as the result of actual discovery. This part of the La Cosa map is easily understood if we assume it to have been drawn as a result of hearsay evidence obtained from the Indians. The Indians told Columbus on his first voyage that Cuba was an island.[36]

From the possible connection of some of the names on the Cantino map with the 1497 voyage of Vespucius, it seems more probable, as is discussed later (pp. 136–138), that this voyage did not extend west-

Footnote 35, continued

idem: Le premier voyage de Amerígo Vespucci définitivement expliqué dans ses détails, Vienna, 1869; *idem:* Nouvelles recherches sur les derniers voyages du navigateur florentin et le reste des documents et éclaircissements sur lui, Vienna, 1870.

[36] Major, *op. cit.*, p. 3 (Raccolta, Part I, Vol. I, p. 122).

ward beyond the Caribbean Sea and that the return was made by way of the Bahamas.

EXAMINATION OF THE VIEWS OF HARRISSE

We may now turn to examine the reasons which have led Harrisse and Thacher to doubt that Columbus believed himself on the coast of Asia in 1502.

The first point urged by Harrisse is expressed as follows:[37]

True it is that, in 1494, he [Columbus] declared, and compelled his crews to affirm before a royal notary, that Cuba was a continent, and that it could be reached by land: . . . As late as 1503, he wrote to Ferdinand and Isabella that he had actually reached the province of Mango, adjoining Cathay:. . . Withal, the appearance is that within himself he thought otherwise. Unfortunately, to acknowledge his doubts in that respect would have been belying the motives of his great enterprise, reducing materially the importance of the results obtained, and leading the Spanish government to discontinue the attempt.

It is true that one school of geographers did deny that Columbus reached Asia; this group followed Ptolemy and did not stretch Asia 45° eastward, as did Marinus and Columbus. It is exactly this 45° difference that separates Asia and the new discoveries of Spain on the Waldseemüller map of 1507.[38] On the other hand, some Spanish authorities believed, in

[37] Harrisse, Discovery of North America, p. 104.
[38] Fischer and von Wieser, work cited above on p. 64, footnote 17.

1513 and even as late as 1540, that the new lands were part of Asia. It was years, in fact, before this idea was entirely abandoned. If that be true, something more than a surmise will be necessary to permit us to set aside the direct evidence that Columbus regarded himself as being on the coast of Asia in 1502.

Again, Harrisse says:[39]

The notions of Columbus concerning the form of the east coast of Asia must have been very clear and positive in his mind, but such only as we find it depicted in all globes and maps, from Ptolemy's to Behaim's. Had he therefore continued to believe that the new lands formed part of the Asiatic continent, his efforts would all have been directed so as to follow simply, northward or southward, the coast of regions which, theoretically at least, were known by every cosmographer. Nor, when Columbus expressed the intention of returning to Spain by way of the East, could he have thought of any other route than the rounding of the Malacca peninsula.

The latter part of this argument has already been dealt with: to go south along the Asiatic coast to India was exactly what Columbus attempted, as will be seen by reference to the map (Pl. II). As for the first part, it is surprising that Harrisse should make such a statement. Anyone who has ever looked at the map of Ptolemy (Fig. 3) knows that he represented land, and not ocean, beyond his farthest known world. Besides, all the early maps of eastern Asia are not alike.

[39] Harrisse, *op. cit.*, p. 105.

The Behaim globe (Fig. 4) and the Martellus map[40] indicate a great peninsula on the southeastern coast of Asia, which does not appear on the Catalan atlas of 1375.[41] Again, the Fra Mauro map of 1459[42] is wholly different from either the Catalan atlas or the Behaim globe as regards the eastern coast. It is really inconceivable that Harrisse should have meant what he said. Of course Columbus had ideas about the eastern coast of Asia; and it would appear that those ideas were very nearly the ideas of Behaim, modified as to longitude.

Furthermore, Harrisse stresses the point that Columbus wrote of the coast of Paria as an immense region hitherto unknown.[43] So it was. It was a Nuevo Mundo, as Fiske points out,[44] and as such it is clearly marked on the Bartholomew Columbus map (Fig. 5)—it was something which had not been described by Marco Polo or anybody else. Columbus never pretended that the Costa de Perlas was Asia. To admit that it was new and hitherto unknown did not in any way affect the question of Honduras being a part of Asia, as viewed by Columbus in 1502. When Pedro de Ledesma declared under oath that Columbus sailed southwest from Jamaica in search of Asia, Harrisse thinks he has positive proof that Columbus did not then believe that he was actually exploring

[40] See, above, p. 64, footnote 15.
[41] See, above, p. 20, footnote 25.
[42] See, above, p. 20, footnote 26.
[43] Harrisse, *op. cit.*, p. 105.
[44] Fiske, *op. cit.*, Vol. 2, p. 117.

the Asiatic coast. By reference to the map (Pl. II) we may, however, see that, if Cuba was Mangi and Honduras was Ciamba, Harrisse's point falls to the ground.

Finally, Harrisse is of opinion[45] that the Asiatic theory involves "the absurd supposition that Columbus believed Asia had two east coasts, one facing Oceanus Indicus, the other facing Oceanus Atlanticus," because he expected to find somewhere a strait that would lead him to the Ganges region. Again, a simple reference to the map is sufficient answer to Harrisse's argument: Asia had an east coast and a south coast; Columbus believed himself on the east coast; he was trying to round the Lochac peninsula, to reach the south coast on the Indian Ocean.

Examination of the Views of Thacher

Thacher is equally positive that Columbus did not believe himself to be on the coast of Asia.[46]

Such a belief, in Thacher's opinion, would have been "contrary to his expression of having found a New World." As has just been pointed out, however, the term "New World," used by Columbus, had reference to the continental mass back of the Costa de Perlas. It had, originally, no reference to the islands and the northern mainland.

[45] Harrisse, *op. cit.*, p. 106.

[46] Thacher, *op. cit.*, Vol. 2, pp. 616–621 (the three quotations are from pp. 617–618).

Again, Thacher argues that this belief would have been "contrary to the information received from the Indians in Veragua, and which he himself accepted as true, that from there westwardly by land was a nine days' journey to another sea, . . . and that this sea would carry him to Cathay or to Catigara." Now the fact is that Columbus did not understand the Indians to say this. He could not and did not confuse the positions of Cathay and Cattigara: Cathay was a great country situated north of Mangi and facing the Eastern Sea—the Atlantic, according to Columbus; Cattigara, on the other hand, was placed by Ptolemy on the southeastern coast of the Indicum Mare and hence was considered by Columbus to be on the opposite side of the great peninsula separating the Eastern from the Indian Sea.

The next point which Thacher brings up is of some importance. The belief, if entertained by Columbus, would, he says, have been "contrary to his knowledge of distances traversed on the surface of the globe both by land and by water." A glance at the Bartholomew Columbus map will indicate as much (Fig. 5). From the first and second voyages it was evident that Cuba and Española were too close to each other to correspond with the accepted relative positions of Mangi and Cipangu, as which they were respectively identified by Columbus. Some compromise had to be made: the Asiatic mainland had either to be moved eastward nearer Española or placed at a greater distance from it, as Bartholomew Columbus did on his map. The distances presented a real difficulty; but the argument loses much of its force if we extend our inquiry to a study of the maps made between 1500 and 1600. In these maps we find both the Spanish and the Portuguese territories displaced, progressively, by too great a longitude. The Portuguese longitudes are too great to the eastward; the Spanish too great to the westward.

Displacement of Longitudes

	Cape of Good Hope	Cape Guardafui	Cape Comorin	Malay Peninsula (Singapore)
Behaim (1492)[47]	12°	20°	——	60°
La Cosa (1500)[48]	——	5°	——	——
Ruysch (1508)[49]	——	12°	15°	40°
Waldseemüller (1507)[50]	——	10°	5°	0°
Ribero (1529)[51]	10°	15°	15°	18°
Cabot (1544)[52]	12°	18°	25°	45°
Ortelius (1570)[53]	10°	10°	15°	10°
Hakluyt (1599)[54]	10°	10°	10°	15°

[47] See, above, p. 59, footnote 7.

[48] See, above, p. 59, footnote 8.

[49] Nordenskiöld, Facsimile-Atlas, Pl. 32.

[50] See, above, p. 64, footnote 17.

[51] Full-size photograph of copy in Grand Ducal Library of Weimar in Portfolio 11 in E. L. Stevenson: Maps Illustrating Early Discovery and Exploration in America, 1502–1530, Reproduced by Photography from the Original Manuscripts, text and 12 portfolios, New Brunswick, N. J., 1903 and 1906. Reduced reproduction of copy in archives of Collegio di Propaganda Fide, Rome, in Nordenskiöld, Periplus, Pls. 48–49.

[52] A photographic facsimile of the original in the Bibliothèque Nationale, Paris, is on the walls of the American Geographical Society of New York (see E. L. Stevenson: A Description of Early Maps, Originals and Facsimiles, 1452–1611, Amer. Geogr. Soc., New York, 1921, pp. 17–18). Also an outline drawing without the legends, reproduced by lithography, in Jomard, op. cit., Pl. XX, 1–4.

[53] Nordenskiöld, Facsimile-Atlas, Pl. 46.

[54] Ibid., Pl. 50.

It will be noticed that in all cases it was contrary to national interest to exaggerate longitude because, after going 180° eastwards or westwards from the Line of Demarcation, the land fell in the sphere of a rival.

When we turn westward across the Atlantic we do not have so clear a case. National interest seems to play a part in placing Brazil and Terra de los Baccalaos (Newfoundland) too far to the eastward, thus bringing more territory within the Portuguese sphere; but even then we have Apianus (1520)[55] placing the Panama region 12° too far westward. Verrazano (1529)[56] placed Terra Nova (Newfoundland) 12° too far to the east, Florida about right, and Vera Cruz 10° too far west. Cabot (1544) displaces Florida westward 12°, eastern Mexico 15°, and Lower California 20°. Ortelius (1570) placed Florida properly and displaced westward Vera Cruz 4° and Lower California 30°. Hakluyt (1599) displaced Florida 5°, Vera Cruz 8°, and Lower California 10° westward at the same time that he corrected the position of Cape Mendocino eastwards by 45°, still leaving it too far west by 25°. It should also be noted that Columbus, in 1494, greatly erred as to the length of Cuba. His 335 leagues would make about 20° as the length of somewhat less than all of the island, whereas its true length is about 10°. One has only to give thought to the extreme difficulty of

[55] *Ibid.*, Pl. 38.
[56] Stevenson, Maps Illustrating Early Discovery, Portfolio 12.

correctly determining longitude without our means of standard time and exact chronometers, and then one marvels at the surprisingly correct results obtained by the great discoverers. In any case, when these facts are carefully studied and the difficulty is envisaged of properly determining distance in an east-west direction at that time much of the force is taken out of Thacher's criticism.

The next point of Thacher's is also of importance. Columbus did not find either great cities or great fleets. Thacher says[57] that "he expected to see none of these things" and that he was simply endeavoring to mystify any pilot who should venture to find his Veragua—as Ojeda and others had done with regard to the Costa de Perlas. We have seen how Columbus was disturbed at not finding the great cities and fleets and how he partially satisfied himself on that score. To prove that Columbus lied to mystify others, Thacher quotes[58] the letter regarding the fourth voyage:

We found ourselves in the land of Maya . . . Let them [the pilots] make known, if they themselves know it, the situation of Veragua. I say that they cannot give other information or account except that they went to some lands where there is much gold and to insist that they did this: but they are ignorant of the route by which to return there and if they were to go there, they would be obliged to make a new discovery of it.

[57] Thacher, *op. cit.*, Vol. 2, p. 621.

[58] *Ibid.*, Vol. 2, p. 618. Cf. Major, *op. cit.*, p. 197 (Raccolta, Part I, Vol. 2, p. 198).

Whatever mystery there was about the location of Veragua, it is certain that the Columbus brothers, Christopher and Bartholomew, shared each other's ideas in regard to the new discoveries, in view of the fact that they had made the fourth voyage together. Bartholomew removed whatever mystery there was when, in Rome after Christopher's death to solicit the assistance of the Pope in persuading the Spanish court to organize a new expedition to colonize the lands discovered on that voyage, he gave friar Jerome of San Giovanni in Laterano a description and map of Veragua, the equivalent of which map von Wieser found on the margin of a copy of Christopher's letter on the fourth voyage written in Jamaica on July 7, 1503.[59] This map (Fig. 5) shows Veragua as a part of Asia. Veragua ("beragnia" on Fig. 5) is a part of an isthmus connecting Asia and Mondo Novo. It separates the Atlantic Ocean from the Magnus Sinus. The map and the letter certainly prove Columbus' Asiatic interpretation of the discoveries on the fourth voyage. The alleged mystification put forward by Thacher is a slight reason, to say the least, on which to throw overboard all the positive assertions of Columbus.

In another place Thacher says:[60]

The reader by this time . . . must be convinced that the Admiral was no longer in doubt as to the character of his discovery. He knew that he had disclosed another

---

[59] von Wieser, *op. cit.*, pp. 4, 5, and 8.
[60] Thacher, *op. cit.*, Vol. 2, p. 568.

continent, and he called it Novus Orbis or Mundus Novus. He knew that the New World lay not in the India of the Old World, but between it and the marts of Europe. He himself had estimated a degree to contain fifty-six and two-thirds miles, and he knew that he must multiply this by three hundred and sixty to circumnavigate the globe. He knew the distance to the extremity of India extra Gangem, as measured eastwardly from the Canaries, on the map of Ptolemy, four editions of whose geography were then already printed and common in the world, and he also knew the distance he had travelled westwardly from the Canaries. He knew that Marco Polo, with whose book he was familiar, since his copy was annotated and marked on many a margin, told of the coast lines of the lands of the Great Khan and of the islands and of powerful peoples out in the China Sea. If he knew all this, he knew that between the country of the Great Khan and the shores of Europe lay great continental lands, and that he—Christopher Columbus —and none other was their discoverer. It is time history erased from its pages that humiliating sentence, "Columbus died believing, not that he had found a new world, but that he had reached the shores of Asia."

In making this statement, Thacher not only ignores the fact that medieval geographers were not agreed on the distance to the extremity of India extra Gangem, but he rejects, apparently, a note of Columbus that he himself has quoted.[61] On the margin of his copy of the "Imago mundi," in the handwriting of Columbus, we read:[62] "A fine Occidentis usque ad

[61] *Ibid.*, Vol. 2, p. 568, note 2.
[62] Raccolta, Part I, Vol. 2, p. 406, No. 486.

American Geogr. Soc. Research Series №14, Pl. II.

:NING THE POSITION OF THE EASTERN COAST OF ASIA IN RELATION TO HIS FOURTH VOYAGE

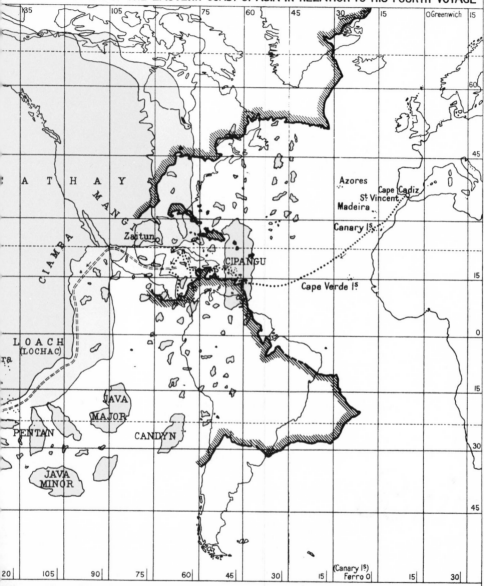

135 105 75 60 45 30 15 0 Greenwich 15

60

45

C A T H A Y

MANG

CIAMBA

Zaitun

CIPANGU

Azores

Cape Cadiz
St Vincent
Madeira

Canary Is

15

Cape Verde Is

0

L O A C H
(LOCHAC)

15

JAVA
MAJOR

PENTAN

CANDYN

30

JAVA
MINOR

45

20 105 90 75 60 45 30 15 (Canary Is) 15 30
Ferro 0

f Asia according to Behaim transposed to
as to bring the cape at Zaitun on same
eastern end of Cuba, which Columbus took for Asia.

according to the world map of Juan de la Cosa
orating the discoveries up to that date.

their true position according to modern maps.

········· Westward route of Columbus on his fourth voyage,
1502–03.

====== Route Columbus believed he was following along the coast
of Asia on his fourth voyage and continuation he
had at one time considered following to reach India.

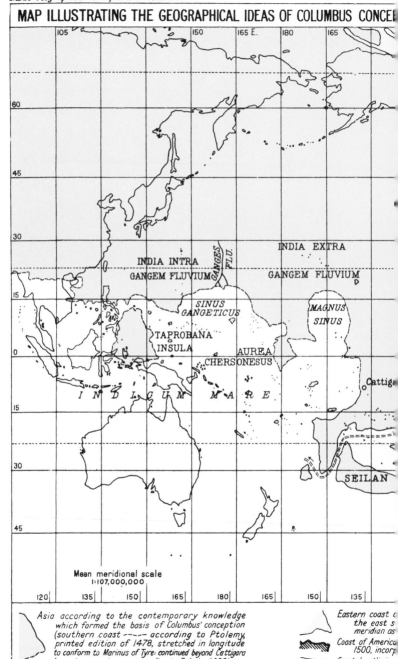

MAP ILLUSTRATING THE GEOGRAPHICAL IDEAS OF COLUMBUS CONCE[R]

INDIA INTRA
GANGEM FLUVIUM

GANGES FLU.

INDIA EXTRA

GANGEM FLUVIUM

SINUS
GANGETICUS

MAGNUS
SINUS

TAPROBANA
INSULA

AUREA
CHERSONESUS

I N D I C U M   M A R E

Cattig[ara]

SEILAN

Mean meridional scale
1:107,000,000

Asia according to the contemporary knowledge
which formed the basis of Columbus' conception
(southern coast ----- according to Ptolemy,
printed edition of 1478, stretched in longitude
to conform to Marinus of Tyre continued beyond Cattigara
by eastern coast —— according to Behaim 1492).

Eastern coast o[f]
the east s[ide]
meridian as

Coast of America[n]
1500, incorp[…]

Coastal outlines

finem Indie per terram est multo plus quam medietas
terre, videlicet gradus 180." According to the geographers, the distance eastward from western Europe
to the farthest known east (Lisbon to the east
coast of China) in degrees of longitude was as follows:[63]

Marinus of Tyre (100 A. D.)	225°
Ptolemy (150)	177°+
Catalan atlas (1375)	116°
Genoese map (1457)	136°
Fra Mauro (1459)	125°
Henricus Martellus (1489)	196°
Laon globe	250°
Behaim (1492)	234°
Columbus (1502)	289°
Actual extent	131°

Of course, the farthest east of Asia included more
land in the later maps than in those of Marinus and
Ptolemy, both of whom understood that there was
more land beyond the farthest known world. One
need only consider for a moment the variants just
cited to realize that neither Columbus nor any one
else in his day knew the distance to the extremity of
India extra Gangem. Instead of knowledge there
was a very wide difference of opinion among those
who had given thought to the subject. Columbus
rejected all the lower figures; and his discoveries had
in a remarkable manner confirmed his estimates.
Had Thacher given due thought to pre-Columbian

[63] Mainly according to Ravenstein, *op. cit.*, p. 64, note 4.

geography he could not have made the assertion that Columbus "knew that the New World lay not in the India of the Old World, but between it and the marts of Europe."

CONCLUSION

To conclude, I feel, after studying the documents cited, after considering the cartographical knowledge that Columbus may have had, and after weighing all that Thacher and Harrisse have to say on the subject, that no evidence has as yet been advanced sufficient to disprove the theory that, in 1502–1503, Columbus believed himself to be on the coast of Asia. Columbus died so believing. After him, Balboa in 1513 so believed. Waldseemüller and the German cartographers did not reject the ideas of Columbus. In a modified form they are embodied in the Schöner globe (1533)[64] and in the Cabot map of 1544. The writings of Castañeda,[65] the chronicler of the Coronado expedition, and the famous Gastaldi map of 1562[66] are further evidence that many of the successors of Columbus continued in the same belief down into the middle of the sixteenth century.

[64] Harrisse, op. cit., facing p. 520.

[65] See G. P. Winship: The Coronado Expedition, 1540–1542, Ann. Rept. Bur. of Amer. Ethnology for 1892–93, Part I, Washington, 1896, pp. 329–613 (Spanish text, pp. 414–469); reference on pp. 512–513 and 525–526.

[66] Nordenskiöld, Periplus, p. 165.

THE IDENTITY OF "FLORIDA" ON THE CANTINO MAP OF 1502

THE PROBLEM STATED

It was long supposed that Ponce de León was the discoverer of Florida. More recently, however, the study of the Cantino, Canerio, and 1507 Waldsee-müller maps,[1] all antedating Ponce's discovery of 1513, has led many scholars to place the honor of

---

[1] The standard reproductions of these maps are as follows:

(1) the Cantino by E. L. Stevenson: Maps Illustrating Early Discovery and Exploration in America, 1502–1530, Reproduced by Photography from the Original Manuscripts, text and 12 portfolios, New Brunswick, N. J., 1903–06, map in Portfolio 1 (the western, Atlantic, half of the map has also been reproduced from a tracing by lithography in the original colors and accompanies in a separate pocket Henry Harrisse: Les Corte-Real et leurs voyages au Nouveau-Monde d'après des documents nouveaux ou peu connus tirés des archives de Lisbonne et de Modène, Paris, 1883, in series: Recueil de Voyages et de Documents Pour Servir à l'Histoire de la Géographie, edit. by C. Schafer and A. Cordier);

(2) the Canerio by E. L. Stevenson: Marine World Chart of Nicolo de Canerio Januensis, 1502 (circa): A Critical Study With Facsimile (text, 1908, and facsimile in portfolio, 1907), Amer. Geogr. Soc. and Hispanic Soc. of America, New York, 1907–08;

(3) the Waldseemüller by Joseph Fischer and F. R. von Wieser: The Oldest Map With the Name America of the Year 1507 and the Carta Marina of the Year 1516 by M. Waldseemüller (Ilacomilus), text in English and German and facsimile of both maps, Innsbruck, 1903.

The same feature appears on maps for years afterwards, such as the following (cf. Harrisse, work cited in next footnote, pp. 371–372):

Waldseemüller gores, 1507 (Fischer and von Wieser, op. cit., p. 14).

Mappemonde of Glareanus, 1510 (A. E. Nordenskiöld: Periplus: An Essay on the Early History of Charts and Sailing-Directions transl. by F. A. Bather, Stockholm, 1897, p. 173).

this achievement upon the brow of some earlier, but unknown, navigator. Each of these three maps (Figs. 8, 9, 12) contains an island, west of Española, occupying the position of Cuba, resembling Cuba in shape, but bearing the name "Ilha yssabella," "Insulla issabella," or "Isabella Insula." Northwest of Isabella is an unnamed peninsular land which has been variously regarded as Asia, Yucatan, Cuba, Florida, and as purely imaginary. The identity of this land is the subject of the present study.

ANALYSIS OF THE PROBLEM BY HARRISSE

The problem presented by this continental land has been analyzed with knowledge and care by Henry

---

Footnote 1, continued

Stobnicza hemispheres, 1512 (*idem:* Facsimile-Atlas to the Early History of Cartography, transl. by J. A. Ekelöf and C. R. Markham, Stockholm, 1889, Pl. 34).

"Admiral's map" in the 1513 Strasburg edition of Ptolemy (Nordenskiöld, Facsimile-Atlas, Pl. 36).

Hauslaub globe, ea. 1510–15 (J. Luksch: Zwei Denkmale alter Kartographie, *Mitt. Geogr. Gesell. in Wien*, Vol. 29, 1886, pp. 364–373; reference on Pl. 5).

Schöner globe, 1515 (F. R. von Wieser: Magalhães-Strasse und Austral-Continent auf den Globen des Johannes Schöner, Innsbruck, 1881, Pl. 2; [E. F.] Jomard: Les monuments de la géographie, ou recueil d'anciennes cartes européennes et orientales . . . Paris, [1842–62], Pl. XVII, reproduced in Nordenskiöld, Facsimile-Atlas, p. 78).

Carta Marina of Waldseemüller, 1516 (Fischer and von Wieser, *op. cit.*).

Schöner globe, 1520 (F. W. Ghillany: Der Erdglobus des Martin Behaim von 1492 und der des Johann Schöner von 1520, Nuremberg, 1842; von Wieser, Magalhães-Strasse, Pl. 1).

Petrus Apianus, 1520 (Nordenskiöld, Facsimile-Atlas, Pl. 38).

Harrisse,[2] and any new discussion must take its departure from his work.

The first supposition in regard to the land northwest of Isabella was, Harrisse points out, that the

[2] Henry Harrisse: The Discovery of North America: A Critical, Documentary and Historic Investigation, London and Paris, 1892, pp. 77–92.

For literature on the Yucatan theory, see Harrisse, p. 80, note 9.

Advocates of the Cuban hypothesis are:

Henry Stevens: Historical and Geographical Notes on the Earliest Discoveries in America, 1453–1530, New Haven, 1869. See also his "Johann Schöner, Professor of Mathematics at Nuremberg," London, 1888, p. xviii.

J. C. Brevoort: Notes on Giovanni da Verrazano and on a Planisphere of 1529 Illustrating His American Voyage in 1524, With a Reduced Copy of the Map, Bull. Amer. Geogr. Soc., Vol. 4, 1873, pp. 145-297 (also published separately under the title "Verrazano the Navigator," New York, 1874); reference on p. 210.

The identification of the land in question with Florida and the eastern coast of North America is maintained by:

F. A. de Varnhagen: Vespuce et son premier voyage, Paris, 1858. See also his "Amerígo Vespucci: Son caractère, ses écrits (même les moins authentiques), sa vie et ses navigations," Lima, 1865.

J. G. Kohl: A History of the Discovery of the East Coast of North America, Particularly the Coast of Maine, from the Northmen in 990 to the Charter of Gilbert in 1578, constituting Vol. 1 of the "Documentary History of the State of Maine" (Collections of the Maine Historical Society, 2nd Series), Portland, 1869, pp. 149 and 236–239.

H. H. Bancroft: Central America (History of the Pacific States of North America, Vols. 1–3), 3 vols., San Francisco, 1882–87; reference in Vol. 1, pp. 99–107.

John Fiske: The Discovery of America, With Some Account of Ancient America and the Spanish Conquest, 2 vols., Boston, 1892; reference in Vol. 2, pp. 74–82.

Harrisse, op. cit., pp. 77–92. See also his "Découverte et évolution cartographique de Terre-Neuve et des pays circonvoisins, 1497, 1501, 1769," London and Paris, 1900, pp. 3–75.

C. R. Markham, transl. and edit.: The Journal of Christopher Columbus (During His First Voyage, 1492–93) and Documents Relating to the Voyages of John Cabot and Gaspar Corte Real, Hakluyt Soc. Publs., 1st Series, Vol. 86, London, 1893, p. xlvii.

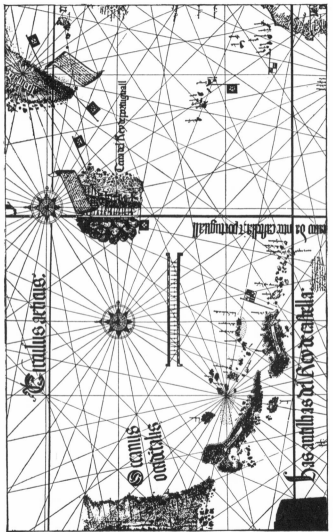

Fig. 8—The North Atlantic area on the Cantino world map of 1502 (from the photographic facsimile in Harrisse's Discovery of North America. Pl. 6).

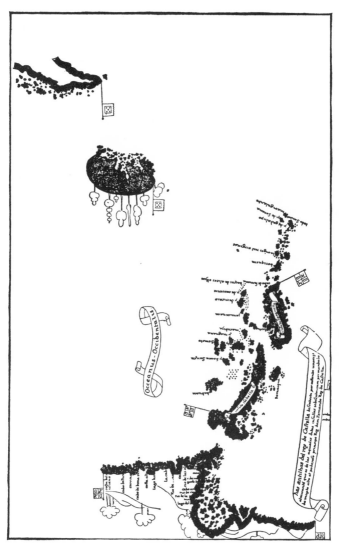

Fig. 9—The North Atlantic area on the Canerio world map of about 1504 (from the hand-copied reproduction in Kretschmer's Atlas zur Entdeckung Amerikas, Pl. 8).

coast line might be a continuation of the eastern seaboard of Asia. He rejects this surmise because the Asiatic coast is depicted in its proper place on the right-hand side of the Cantino map, as it also is on the Canerio and Waldseemüller maps.

The second hypothesis was that the land was Yucatan, inserted upside down "by some unaccountable mistake of the cartographer." Harrisse rejects this view on the grounds that Yucatan was not known until 1517 and that the configuration of the two does not at all coincide.

The theory that the land was purely imaginary cannot, Harrisse thinks, be entertained in presence of the fact that along the coast there are as many as twenty-two place names (quoting Kohl) "such as a

Footnote 2, continued

E. G. Bourne: Spain in America, 1450–1580 (The American Nation: A History, Vol. 3), New York, 1904, p. 61.

E. L. Stevenson: Martin Waldseemüller and the Early Lusitano-Germanic Cartography of the New World, *Bull. Amer. Geogr. Soc.*, Vol. 36, 1904, pp. 193–215; reference on p. 200. See also his "Typical Early Maps of the New World," *ibid.*, Vol. 39, pp. 202–224, reference on p. 207; his "Marine World Chart of Nicolo de Canerio," already cited, text, p. 32; and his Early Spanish Cartography of the New World, With Special Reference to the Wolfenbüttel-Spanish Map and the Work of Diego Ribero, *Proc. Amer. Antiquarian Soc.*, Worcester, Mass., Vol. 19 (N. S.), 1909, pp. 369–419, reference on p. 395.

Woodbury Lowery: The Spanish Settlements Within the Present Limits of the United States, 1513–1561, New York and London, 1901, pp. 128–129.

Neutral in the controversy are:

J. G. Shea: Ancient Florida, pp. 231–298 in Vol. 2 of Justin Winsor, edit.: Narrative and Critical History of America, 8 vols., Boston, 1884–89; reference on pp. 231–232.

Justin Winsor: Christopher Columbus, and How He Received and Imparted the Spirit of Discovery, Boston, 1891, pp. 421–426.

navigator might well have distributed on an unknown coast discovered by him."

The Cuban hypothesis is also rejected by Harrisse, after a discussion[3] which, on account of the points it brings up, may be quoted at some length:

Another interpretation has been lately advanced. It is to the effect that the continental coast line which emerges from the north-western side of the Cantino planisphere is Cuba, although that island already figures on the map in its own proper place among the Antilles. Thus far, not a particle of evidence has been adduced in support of the assertion. We will, nevertheless, examine this bare averment with as much care as if it reposed on facts, documents, or cogent reasons.

It will be shown hereafter that, when the Cantino chart was made, cartographers, in Spain as well as in Portugal, properly considered Cuba as an island. They depicted it as such on their maps as early as the year 1500, with many names and an outline sufficiently exact to warrant the belief that the data used by those map-makers were originally obtained *de visu.*

Christopher Columbus at first also believed in the insularity of Cuba, as in his Journal he invariably mentions it as "la isla de Cuba." But he soon afterwards changed his opinion, and, June 12, 1494, compelled his officers and crews to declare that Cuba was a continent. January 14, 1495, and even at a later period, he continued to profess such an erroneous belief. And, as we shall show hereafter, Columbus being alone of that opinion, if the configuration which we are discussing ever was intended to represent the island of Cuba it must have been borrowed from one of his early maps.

[3] Harrisse, Discovery of North America, pp. 83–85.

A priori, such a cartographical operation is not impossible. We are able to realise how a planisphere can have been first constructed, in Lisbon or elsewhere, setting forth the results of Columbus' earliest voyages, and delineating Cuba according to geographical misconceptions which he still maintained in 1495. To this primary map would have been added, several years afterwards, the Venezuelan and Brazilian coasts, borrowed from charts brought by Hojeda or La Cosa, Niño or Guerra, Cabral or De Lemos, and the pilots of Gaspar Corte-Real who returned to Lisbon in October, 1501. We should thus have the prototype of the Cantino and of all early Portuguese charts. But is the Cantino planisphere such a map? That is the question. We propose to show that it is not, never was, and never could be.

In the first place, a map of that description could not have exhibited the continental outline assumed to be Cuba and, at the same time, the island of that name, depicted insularily, and placed where it lies in reality, between Hispaniola and the American continent. It is evident that if Columbus and those who actually shared the opinion—if there were any such in 1502—did not believe in the existence of the *island* of Cuba, they could not have inscribed it on their charts. Then it is difficult to conceive how cartographers or mariners, including Columbus himself in 1495 or at any time, could have given to the region which they called Cuba, even when assuming it to be a continent, a shape so different from the true form of the portions of the island actually seen and surveyed by them, however incomplete may have been their knowledge of its configuration. Nor could they have represented their supposed Cuba as running from *south to north,* over a space covering more than twenty degrees of latitude.

The reason for such an impossibility is obvious. In November, 1492, the great Genoese had ranged the northern coast of that island, first on the north side, westward, beyond Nuevitas del Principe; then eastward as far as Cape Maysi; and in the summer of 1494 on the south side, from its eastern extremity to beyond what he called the Isla Evangelista, which, Las Casas says, is the Isla de Pinos. It follows that when Columbus depicted Cuba, assuming that he gave it a continental aspect, he must have represented that region, so early as 1494 or 1495, not as it is on the Cantino chart, viz: in the shape of a continent extending straight from south to north, but, on the contrary, in the form of a long peninsula, running *from east to west,* and for a very great distance, as he claimed to have coasted the region *westward* more than three hundred and thirty-five leagues . . . a statement which is hyperbolical, as the entire length of the island from east to west is only two hundred and thirty-five leagues, but which implies nevertheless a considerable ranging of the Cuban coast.

Nor, when coming to depict the point where the peninsula was supposed to be soldered to the continent, would Columbus or his followers have made the coast line trend due north, and especially for a distance embracing at least twenty degrees of latitude. On the contrary, his coast could but run *southward,* for such was his decided opinion, clearly expressed in June, 1494. Speaking of the alleged western terminus of Cuba, Columbus said: "From this point onward, the coast extends southwardly" . . . and he compelled all his pilots, Francisco Niño, Alonso Medel, Bartolomé Perez,

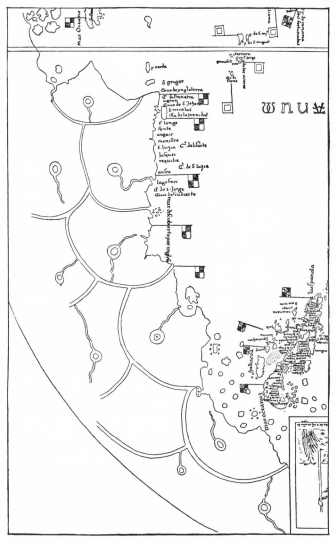

Fig. 10—The North Atlantic area on Juan de la Cosa's world map of 1500 (from the hand-copied reproduction in Kretschmer's Atlas zur Entdeckung Amerikas, Pl. 7).

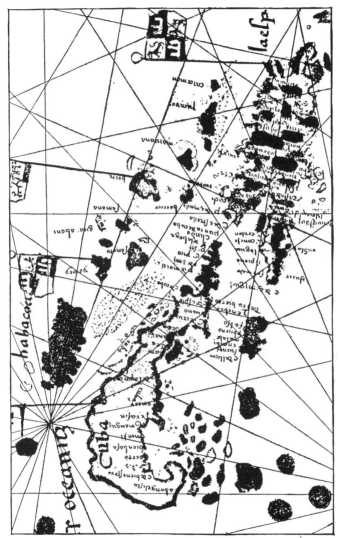

Fig. 11—Cuba and Española on the La Cosa map (from the photographic enlargement in Harrisse's Discovery of North America, Pl. 7).

and even La Cosa himself, to declare that "from there the country turned south and south-west." . . . Peter Martyr in his epistle of August 9, 1495, reports having received a letter from Columbus stating that "the shores of Cuba trend so much to the southward that he thought himself at times very near the equator." Now, instead of this alleged south coast, the Cantino chart at that point marks a right angle and runs due west; which proves that this configuration contradicts even the erroneous cosmographical hypothesis advanced by Columbus.

In the foregoing quotation Harrisse gives certain reasons for believing that the unknown land was not Cuba. He then proceeds to maintain the same conclusion from a consideration of place names. In this he compares[4] the nomenclature of the northwestern continental region on the Cantino map from his own reproduction (Fig. 14) with the names given to geographical features along the coast of Cuba by Columbus, as reported by himself[5] and by his con-

[4] Harrisse, *op. cit.*, p. 86.

[5] In his letter on the first voyage, dated Feb. 15, 1493, with postscript of March 4, 1493, in Raccolta di documenti e studi pubblicati dalla R. Commissione Colombiana pel Quarto Centenario dalla Scoperta dell' America (6 parts in 14 vols., Rome, 1892–96), Part I, Vol. 1, pp. 120–135. Also in modernized Spanish(after Navarrete,Vol. 1, pp.167–195; see below, footnote 17), with English translation, in R. H. Major, transl. and edit.: Select Letters of Christopher Columbus, With Other Original Documents, Relating to His Four Voyages to the New World, 2nd edit., *Hakluyt Soc. Publs.*, 1st Series, Vol. 43, London, 1870, pp. 1–18. Also, with regard to the first and second voyages, to the extent that his own words are quoted in the accounts of his contemporaries, cited in the next three footnotes.

The coast of Cuba was charted and names were given to its geographical features on the first and second voyages. On the first voyage, from Oct. 28 to Dec. 5, 1492, the eastern part of the northern coast was outlined, from about Guajaba Key (77½° W.) to Cape Maisi. On the

temporary historians, Las Casas,[6] Bernáldez,[7] and Ferdinand Columbus.[8] The two lists, as given by Harrisse, are as follows:

Northwest coast in the map of Cantino	*Description of Cuba by Columbus, Bernáldez, Las Casas, and in the "Historie"*
Rio de las palmas	Rio (and) Puerto San Sal-
Rio do corno	vador
C. arlear	Rio de la Luna
G. do lurcor	Rio de Mares (or) de Mari
C. do mortinbo	Peña de los Enamorados[9]
C. lurcar	Cabo de Palmas
El golfo bavo	Rio del Sol
C. do fim do abrill	Cabo de Cuba

second voyage, from April 30 to May 3, 1494, the southern coast was followed, first from Cape Maisi to a point opposite Jamaica and then, on the return from that island, from May 15 to July 22, from Cape Cruz for almost the entire distance westward to a point northwest of the Isle of Pines and back again to Cape Cruz.

[6] Bartolomé de las Casas: Historia de las Indias, 5 vols., Madrid, 1875–76; references in Book I, Chs. 44–50 and 94–97 (Vol. 1, pp. 318–361, and Vol. 2, pp. 49–67).

[7] Andrés Bernáldez: Historia de los Reyes Católicos D. Fernando y Da. Isabel, 2 vols., Seville, 1870 (also Granada, 1856); references in Vol. 1, pp. 357–369, and Vol. 2, pp. 42–82.

[8] Vita di Cristoforo Colombo descritta da Ferdinando, suo figlio, London, 1867 (in English in Churchill's "A Collection of Voyages and Travels," Vol. 2), Chs. 26–29 (i. e. 27–30) and 53–58 (i. e. 54–59). For bibliographical details, see footnote 6 in the second study, p. 36, above.

[9] Columbus does not give this as a name; he merely states that the mountains are *like* the Peña de los Enamorados near Granada. See the Journal under date of Oct. 29, 1492 (Raccolta, Part I, Vol. 1, p. 32; translated in Markham, *op. cit.*, p. 62) and Las Casas, *op. cit.*, Book I, Ch. 44 (Vol. 1, p. 319).—G. E. N.

Cornejo
Rio de dõ diego
C. delgato
Punta [Pũta] Roixa
Rio de las Almadias
Cabo Santo
Rio de los largartos
Las cabras
Lago luncor
Costa alta
Cabo de b . . a bentura
Canju . . .
Cabo d. licõtu
Costa del mar vçiano

Mar de Nuestra Señora
Puerto del Principe
Puerto de Santa Catalina
Cabo del Pico
Cabo de Campana
Puerto Santo
Cabo Lindo
Cabo del Monte
Alpha y Omega
Puerto grande
Puerto bueno[10]
Cabo de Cruz
Jardin de la Reina
Isla Sancta Maria
Isla Evangelista
Punta del Serafin

The conclusion to which Harrisse comes, on the basis of this comparison, is that "there is not a single name" in the nomenclature of the continental region which figures at all in any of the lists ascribed to the island of Cuba by Columbus and the chroniclers of his voyages. The continental land and the island of Cuba cannot, therefore, he says, be one and the same.

In a similar way, he compares[11] the Cantino names with those of La Cosa as interpreted by von Hum-

[10] This name was given, on the second voyage, to a harbor in Jamaica, not in Cuba. Cf. Las Casas, *op. cit.*, Book I, Ch. 94 (Vol. 2, p. 52) and Ferdinand Columbus, *op. cit.*, Ch. 54 (i. e. 55), p. 163.—G. E. N.

[11] Harrisse, Discovery of North America, p. 91.

boldt,[12] de la Sagra,[13] Jomard,[14] and from a photograph (twice the size of the original)[15] taken directly
from the original at Madrid in 1890 (Fig. 11). The
comparative list, as given by Harrisse, is as follows:[16]

[12] Alexander von Humboldt: Examen critique de l'histoire de la géographie du nouveau continent et des progrès de l'astronomie nautique
aux quinzième et seizième siècles, 5 vols., Paris, 1836–39; reference in
Vol. 5, Pl. 33 (American section of map on half the scale of the original)
and Pl. 34 (Caribbean section on original scale).

[13] Ramón de la Sagra: Historia física, política y natural de la isla de
Cuba, Part I: Historia física y política, 2 vols., Paris, 1842, Pl. 1 at end
of Vol. 2.

[14] Jomard, op. cit., Pl. XVI, 1, 2, 3.

[15] Harrisse, op. cit., Pl. 7, facing p. 91. The official facsimile of the
map in the original colors, edited by Cánovas Vallejo and Traynor,
accompanies Antonio Vascáno: Ensayo biográfico del célebre navegante
y consumado cosmógrafo Juan de la Cosa y descripción é historia de su
famosa carta geográfica, Madrid, 1892, text in Spanish, French, and
English. The reproductions by von Humboldt, de la Sagra, and Jomard
cited in the preceding footnotes are in black and white. That by
Jomard is of the whole map on the original scale (there is a reduced
reproduction of the whole map in A. E. Nordenskiöld, Periplus, Pls.
43–44). Those by von Humboldt and de la Sagra are of the American
sections only.

[16] Reference to the cited reproductions themselves of the La Cosa map
show a number of minor discrepancies between Harrisse's transcription
of the names and the names as they appear on the reproductions. Thus,
on the Humboldt reproduction "Sipica" reads "Sipione" and, like
(C° de S.) Miguel refers to Española, not to Cuba. "Entubi" refers to
Jamaica. "Matata" reads "Macata." The following names, which
have equivalents in the De la Sagra or Jomard lists, appear in Humboldt's full-size reproduction but are omitted by Harrisse: Bienbaso,
Fumos, C°. Negro, C°. de Cuba, Rio de la Vega. On the De la Sagra
reproduction "sexto" follows "bien baja" and "junez" follows "P. del
Principe," to use the order of Harrisse's list. On the Jomard reproduction, on which the lettering is not always easy to decipher, Harrisse's
"fuma" reads "luna" and "fumos" follows "cuba" in the order of
Harrisse's list.

Cantino (original)	La Cosa (Photo) [our Fig. 11]	La Cosa (Humboldt)	La Cosa (De la Sagra)	La Cosa (Jomard)
Rio de las palmas	punta de cuba	Ponta de cuba	Punta de Cuba	ponta de Cuba
Rio do corno	clindo	Sipica	Clindo	Cliuda
C. arlear	r° de la bega	Miguel	r° de la bega	r° de la bega
G. do lurcor	p° sté		psto	p. sto
C. do mortinbo	C. pico	C. Pico	O pico	C. pico
C. lurcar	p. de s. mj.	Entubi	p. de S. my	p. de S. mi°
el golfo bavo	p. de maici	P. de Maiti	p. de maiti	p. de main
C. do fim do abrill	C. de cuba		C. de Cuba	C. de Cuba
Cornejo	C. de espto		C. de espitto	C. de espera
Rio de dõ diego	C. bueno			C. de au bueno
C. delgato	C. de cruz	C. de Cruz	C. de onez	
Punta Roixa	?		nov	solor
Rio de las Almaidas [sic]	... ana ... (?)	Matata		
Cabo Santo	... sea ... (?)	Conia	Conia	fuma

Cantino (original)	La Cosa (Photo) [our Fig. 11]	La Cosa (Humboldt)	La Cosa (De la Sagra)	La Cosa (Jomard)
Rio de los largartos	Cuba	Cuba		
las cabras	. . . am . . . (?)		C. negro	magno ma ica
lago luncor	r° de las piedras (?)	La Pieta	P. del Principe	del pieta
costa alta	cuba			cuba
cabo de bõa ventura	ancon (?)		sexto	baxi
cansure	serafin	Serafin	C. serafin	serafin
cabo d. licotu	C. manguj	C. Man-guin	C. mang-ny	C. maug-ny
costa del mar uçiano	mensi (?)		junez	fumos
	bien basa cerro (?)		bien baja	bien baso oerto bordoe
	C. de bien espera	C. Bien Espera	C. de bien espero	C. de bien espera
	abange-lista	Abange-lista	Abange-lista	abanar-lista

Again Harrisse points out there is not in La Cosa's Cuba, any more than in the nomenclature and description of Las Casas, Bernáldez, Ferdinand Columbus, and Christopher Columbus himself, *a single one* of the twenty-two names which are inserted on the northwestern continental region of the Cantino chart.

THE PROBLEM RECONSIDERED

The arguments of Harrisse place the problem fairly before us. With his conclusions the present writer takes issue. The problem of the continental land will, therefore, be considered anew in respect to (1) the shape depicted; (2) the names derived from Columbus; (3) the names possibly derived from other sources; (4) doubtful names; and, finally (5), the geographical theories which led to the location of the region northwest of the so-called island of Isabella.

THE SHAPE OF THE LAND

The shape of the land seems to have been derived from statements concerning the coasts discovered on the second voyage of Columbus. In the "Información y testimonio" of Fernand Perez de Luna, concerning the oath taken by the pilots and crew to the effect that Cuba was a continental land, is a passage[17] that seems to be the origin of the shape of the land as it appears on the Cantino map:

[17] J. B. Thacher: Christopher Columbus: His Life, His Work, His Remains, 3 vols., New York, 1903–04; reference in Vol. 2, p. 327 (Spanish text and English translation, the former from M. F. de Navarrete: Relaciones, cartas y otros documentos concernientes á los cuatro viages que hizo el Almirante D. Cristóbal Colón para el descubrimiento de las Indias occidentales, Madrid, 1825; and *idem:* Colección de documentos

Don Christopher Columbus . . . required me, Fernand Perez de Luna, one of the Public Notaries of the City of Isabella,[18] on the part of their Highnesses: that inasmuch as he had left the said City of Isabella with three caravels to come and discover the continental land of the Indies, although he had already discovered part of it on the other voyage which he had first made here the past year of the Lord 1493, and had not been able to learn the truth in regard to it: because although he travelled a long distance beside it, he had not found persons on the seacoast who were able to give a trustworthy account of it, because they were all naked people who did not possess property of their own nor trade, nor go outside their houses, nor did others come to them, according to what he learned from them: and on this account he did not declare affirmatively that it was the continental land, except that he pronounced it doubtful, and had named it *La Juana* in memory of the Prince Don Juan, our Lord: and now he left the said city of Isabella the 24th day of the month of April and came to seek the land of the said *Juana* nearest to the island of Isabella,[19] which is shaped like a triangle extending from east to west, and the point is the eastern part, twenty-two leagues from Isabella . . . (la cual es fecha como un giron que va de Oriente á Occidente, y la punta está de la parte del Oriente propinca á la Isabela veinte é dos leguas).

concernientes á la persona, viages y descubrimientos del Almirante D. Cristóbal Colón, Madrid, 1825, forming Vols. 1 and 2 of his "Colección de los viages y descubrimientos que hicieron por mar los Españoles desde fines del siglo XV," 5 vols., Madrid, 1825–37; reference in Vol. 2, Document 76 on pp. 143–149).

[18] On the northern coast of the island of Haiti.—G. E. N.

[19] The fourth island discovered by Columbus on his first voyage, one of the Bahamas.—G. E. N.

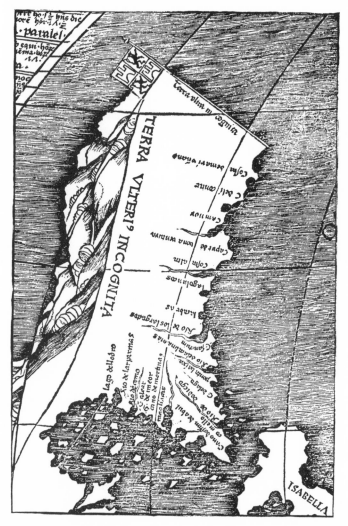

Fig. 12—The northwestern land on the Waldseemüller map of 1507 (from the facsimile in Fischer and von Wieser's The Oldest Map With the Name America, Pl. 2).

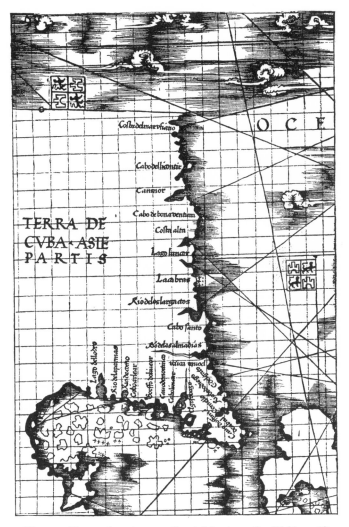

Fig. 13—The northwestern continental land on the Waldseemüller map of 1516 (from the facsimile in Fischer and von Wieser's The Oldest Map With the Name America, Pl. 15).

This statement must be taken in connection with others relating to the first voyage. Regarding the land discovered, Columbus said:[20]

. . . I thought it must be the mainland—the province of Cathay; and, as I found neither towns nor villages on the sea-coast but only a few hamlets, with the inhabitants of which I could not hold conversation because they all immediately fled, I kept on the same route, thinking that I could not fail to light upon some large cities and towns. At length, after the proceeding of many leagues, and finding that nothing new presented itself, and that the coast was leading me northwards. . . .

Again, Martin Alonso Pinzón reported[21] to Columbus on October 30, 1492, that he believed "the land was the mainland and went far to the north and was very great" (y que toda aquella tierra era tierra firme, pues iba tanto al Norte y era tan grande). Furthermore, according to Las Casas,[21a] Columbus found the latitude to be 42° N. Las Casas is suspicious of this value, and justly so, for it should be 21° N., and ascribes it to a slip of the pen. The discrepancy is, however, explained, as Navarrete points out,[21b] by the fact that the quadrants of the time were graduated to half degrees. Nevertheless, it is probable that this erroneous latitude influenced the maker of the Cantino map.

[20] Raccolta, Part I, Vol. 1, p. 121; Major, *op. cit.*, pp. 2–3.

[21] Las Casas, *op. cit.*, Book I, Ch. 44, (Vol. 1, p. 322); and journal of the first voyage, in entry for Oct. 30, 1492 (Raccolta, Part I, Vol. 1, p. 32; Markham, *op. cit.*, p. 63).

[21a] Las Casas, *op. cit.*, Book 1, Chs. 44 and 45 (references in Vol. 1, pp. 324 and 328.) [21b] Navarrete, *op. cit.*, Vol. 1, p. 44, note 5.

Now let us consider these facts. There was supposed to be a mainland called Juana by Columbus. This land was shaped, as far as known, like a triangle. The southern coast ran east and west. The eastern coast ran to the north. It was twenty-two leagues from the eastern end of the land to Isabella. Española was not mentioned in the "Información y testimonio" in connection with the position of the triangle.

Turning now to the Cantino map (Fig. 8), we find that these facts are obviously incorporated in it: the coast of the northwestern mainland is shaped like a triangle and the island of Isabella is placed to the east between the mainland and Española. Cuba does not appear; but on the Waldseemüller map of 1516,[22] which, judging from shape and names, follows the same source as the Cantino map, we find on the triangular mainland the legend "Terra de Cuba Asie Partis" (Fig. 13). Here, then, we have the clue that unravels the mystery that is a stumbling block to Harrisse—Columbus and his companions were the unconscious source of the error, though they themselves could not imaginably have represented the geography of the New World as did Cantino. In short, the error is due to the interpretation put upon the descriptions of Columbus by cartographers who had not been on the ground and who were endeavoring to harmonize conflicting data as best they might.

[22] Fischer and von Wieser, *op. cit.*

If, now, we look further, we find on the Canerio chart,[23] possibly of a little later date than the Cantino, that, on the triangular mainland west of what would correspond to the farthest navigation on the southern coast of Cuba made by Columbus on his second voyage, the land turns southward and a delta with three openings appears there as a conspicuous feature of the coast (Fig. 9). Corresponding with this feature, Peter Martyr states,[24] in his account of the fourth voyage of Columbus, "that within a distance of eight leagues he discovered three rivers of clear water, upon whose banks grew canes as thick round as a man's leg." The Canerio delta, according to Varnhagen,[25] is that of the Mississippi; but, if intended for the Mississippi, it strangely appears on the western instead of the northern coast of the gulf. If, however, this continental land represents Cuba, which Columbus believed to be the mainland of Asia (as on the configuration of the Behaim globe[26] and the Martellus map[27]), then all is clear and simple. As we have seen in the preceding study (p. 70 and Pl. II), the northeastern coast of Cuba was the eastern coast of Cathay; the southern

[23] See, above, footnote 1. For other reproductions see those mentioned below in footnote 31, second paragraph. The date of this map is uncertain. Stevenson dates it about 1502; the writer believes it is not earlier than 1504.

[24] F. A. MacNutt, transl. and edit.: De Orbe Novo: The Eight Decades of Peter Martyr D'Anghera, 2 vols., New York, 1912; reference in Vol. 1, p. 319.

[25] Varnhagen, Vespuce, p. 30.

[26] E. G. Ravenstein: Martin Behaim, His Life and His Globe, London, 1908, with facsimile of gores of globe.

[27] Reproduced in Nordenskiöld, Periplus, p. 123.

coast was the southern coast of Mangi; and westward the coast should, theoretically, turn south; the land to the west was Ciamba. The southward turn of the Cuban coast was taken in the summer of 1494 as a proof that Cuba was part of the Asiatic mainland.[28] The fourth voyage of Columbus was conducted on the same theory.

THE PLACE NAMES CONSIDERED

In turning to consider the names on the continental land, we are met with a most curious error on the part of Harrisse. When he compares the names on the Cantino chart with the nomenclature of Columbus (pp. 103–104) he starts, in the case of the latter, with the name at the northern end of the eastern coast and follows the names in order south, and then west along the southern coast;[29] when, however, he takes up the Cantino chart, he starts with the name at the western end of the southern coast and goes east and then north—in the reverse order to what he did in the first instance. As a result he finds there

[28] Letter of Columbus on the third voyage (Raccolta, Part I, Vol. 2, pp. 26–40, reference on p. 27; translation in Major, *op. cit.*, pp. 108–151, reference on p. 110); testimony of Fernand Perez de Luna (Navarrete, *op. cit.*, Vol. 2, Document 76 on pp. 143–149, reference on p. 144; translation in Thacher, *op. cit.*, Vol. 2, pp. 327–333, reference on p. 329); Fiske, *op. cit.*, Vol. 1, pp. 476–477; Stevens, Historical and Geographical Notes, p. 12.

[29] Strictly, Harrisse lists these names in the chronological order of discovery; except for the first four names (exclusive of Peña de los Enamorados; see, above, footnote 9), given on the first voyage, this coincides with the topographical order here indicated.

is not a single name to correspond in the two lists. In setting forth the names on the La Cosa map (p. 106), he starts with the Punta de Cuba and goes north, after which he returns to the same point and goes west.

If, now, we reverse one of these lists, and so take the names in the same order in each case and compare the Cantino and La Cosa names as well as the names and descriptions of the

Fig. 14—The northwestern continental land on the Cantino map (from the hand-copied reproduction accompanying Harrisse's Les Corte-Real).

For general relation, see Fig. 8.

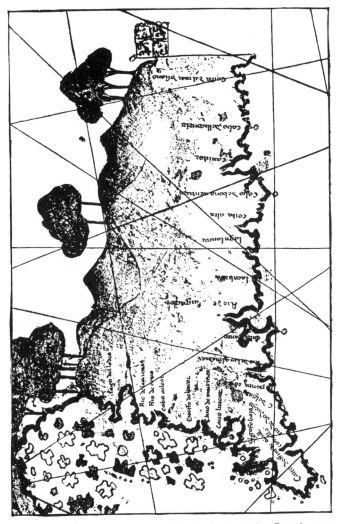

Fig. 15—The northwestern continental land on the Canerio map (enlarged from the photographic facsimile in Harrisse's Discovery of North America, Pl. 14). For general relation, see Fig. 9.

coast given by Columbus, as reported by himself and his contemporary historians,[30] a sufficient number of the names can be identified to establish a vital connection between the Cantino mainland and the explorations of Columbus on the first and second voyages. The method to be followed will be to take the names on the Cantino map[31] (Fig. 14) and search for their equivalents. The starting point will be the first name at the north on the eastern coast and thence around to the last name on the southern coast at the west.

NAMES DERIVED FROM THE VOYAGES OF COLUMBUS

(A) EASTERN COAST

Costa del mar vçiano: On the northern side of the island of Cuba La Cosa names the water "Mar Oceanuz." It is not a great change to name the coast facing this sea the Costa del Mar Vçiano.

[30] See, above, footnotes 5–8.

[31] On Stevenson's photograph of the Cantino map (see footnote 1, above) the names are hard to read because, on the photograph, the coloring of the land often obscures the lettering. For this reason the names as they appear on the hand-traced facsimile in Harrisse's "Les Corte-Real" (see footnote 1), reproduced in our Fig. 14, are used in the present analysis.

On the other hand, on Stevenson's excellent heliotype facsimile of the Canerio map on the scale of the original the names are easily legible, and this reproduction has, therefore, been used, in preference to the facsimile of a part by Harrisse (Discovery of North America, Pl. 14; however, used, for our Fig. 15 for technical reasons) and to the much-reduced facsimile of the whole by Gabriel Marcel (Reproductions de cartes et de globes relatifs à la découverte de l'Amérique du XVI⁰ au XVIII⁰ siècle, text and atlas, Paris, 1893; reference in atlas, Pls. 2 and 3). Interpretations (not facsimiles) of the names are available on the reproductions

Canfure: Possibly "city of the Can," or "Can fu." This name occurs in the region where Columbus sent two of his men with a letter to endeavor to find the Great Khan (Can) on the northern coast of Cuba.[32] The Canerio map has the name "Caninor" (Fig. 15); Waldseemüller (1507), "Camnor" (Fig. 12). These names seem to relate to the same incident as above and occur on the same part of the coast.

Costa alta: The "high coast," a name most certainly not applicable to any point on the coast of Florida, the Carolinas, Virginia, or the Jersey coast. If, however, we turn to the account by Las Casas of the first voyage of Columbus, we find under October 28 the observation:[33] "He says the island is full of very beautiful but not very high mountains and all the rest of the land seemed to him like the island of

by Gallois (Une nouvelle carte marine du XVIe siècle: Le portulan de Nicolas de Canerio, *Bull. Soc. de Géogr. de Lyon*, Vol. 9, 1890, pp. 97–190, 2 plates, and Konrad Kretschmer: Die Entdeckung Amerikas in ihrer Bedeutung für die Geschichte des Weltbildes, 2 vols. (text and atlas), Berlin, 1892; reference in atlas, Pl. 8 (our Fig. 9).

Although the facsimile of the La Cosa map by Cánovas Vallejo and Traynor (see footnote 15) is the official reproduction, the color lithography in which it is printed is not refined enough to bring out all names clearly. Harrisse's reproduction of the photographic enlargement of Cuba on this map (Discovery of North America, Pl. 7; our Fig. 11), which is satisfactory, has therefore here been used.

[32] Letter on the first voyage (Raccolta, Part I, Vol. 1, p. 124; translation in Major, *op. cit.*, p. 3); Journal (Raccolta, Part I, Vol. 1, pp. 34–36; translation in Markham, *op. cit.*, pp. 66–69).

[33] Las Casas, *op. cit.*, Book I, Ch. 44 (Vol. 1, p. 320). The corresponding passage in the Journal reads (Raccolta, Part I, Vol. 1, p. 31; transl. in Markham, *op. cit.*, p. 60): la isla dize qu'es llena de montañas muy hermosas, aunque no son muy grandes en longura, salvo altas, y toda la otra tierra es alta de la manera de Cecilia.

Sicily, high" (Decia ser la isla llena de montañas muy hermosas, aunque no muy altas, y toda la otra tierra le parecia como la isla de Cecilia, alta).

lago luncor: Las Casas, under date of November 3, says[34] that the "Admiral entered a boat to see that river which made with its mouth a great lake and thus constituted a most excellent deep and rock-free port" (Sábado, 3 dias de Noviembre, por la mañana, entró el Almirante en la barca por ver aqual rio, el cual hace á la boca un gran lago, y deste se constituye un singularísimo puerto muy hondo y limpio de piedras). This description is applied to that part of Cuba which was seen six days after the Costa alta. The meaning of the word "luncor" is not known; possibly it was meant for "lago luengo,"[35] or long lake. The lago is quite possibly the one referred to above.

las cabras: This name, "the goats," is almost certainly a corruption. Goats are not native to the American continent. It is reasonably certain that none of the early discoverers of the eastern part of America saw any goats. On the other hand, if we turn to the account of the first voyage, we find the following statement under the date of November 29 :[36] "The sailors also found, in one house, the head of a man in a basket, covered with another basket, and

[34] Las Casas, *op. cit.*, Book I, Ch. 45 (Vol. 1, p. 328).

[35] Fiske, *op. cit.*, Vol. 2, p. 78.

[36] Raccolta, Part I, Vol. 1, p. 52 (transl. in Markham, *op. cit.*, p. 92, under entry incorrectly dated Nov. 27); Las Casas, *op. cit.*, Book I, Ch. 48 (Vol. 1, p. 354).

fastened to a post of the house" (Hallaron también los marineros en casa una cabeça de hombre dentro en un cestillo, cubierto con otro cestillo, y colgado de un poste de la casa). This episode seems to be the basis of the name "las cabras." Some sailor in attempting to make a map of the coast of Cuba may have written "cabzas" for "cabezas," omitting the *e;* the *z* was then taken by the Cantino chart-maker for an *r*, in order to make sense, hence "las cabras."

Rio de los largartos: This name seems to be an interpolation either from the first voyage of Columbus, at the time he was visiting the island he named Isabella, or from the second voyage while he was coasting the southern shore of Cuba. Apparently, the Spaniards saw their first iguana on the island of Isabella, and it was described by Columbus.[37] The name "Rio de los largartos" may have been transferred to the island of Cuba and then carried over, along with the other names, from the real Cuba to the mainland in the Cantino map. There is, however, another possibility. Speaking of the second voyage, both Andrés Bernáldez and Peter Martyr[38] refer to the Spaniards landing on the southern coast

[37] Journal under date of Oct. 21, 1492 (Raccolta, Part I, Vol. 1, p. 27; transl. in Markham, *op. cit.*, p. 54). See also Las Casas, *op. cit.*, Book I, Ch. 43 (Vol. 1, pp. 313–314 and 316) and Paesi novamente retrovati & Novo Mondo da Alberico Vesputio Florentino intitulato [1508], reproduced in facsimile from the McCormick-Hoe copy in the Princeton University Library (Vespucci Reprints, Texts and Studies, VI), Princeton, N. J., 1916, p. 105.

[38] Bernáldez, *op. cit.*, Seville edition, Vol. 2, pp. 46–47; MacNutt, *op. cit.*, Vol. 1, pp. 94–95. See also Paesi novamente retrovati, p. 116.

of Cuba and finding the Indians preparing a meal of fish and serpents, which latter Bernáldez describes in such a way as to make certain that they were iguanas. Peter Martyr describes the serpents as eight feet long and in no wise different from the crocodiles of the Nile except in point of size. *Lagarto* (from the Latin *lacertus*) is the Spanish form of the word lizard. The iguana belongs to the lizard family. The name "Rio de los largartos," if due to the above incident on the second vóyage, may have been transferred to the northern coast by being written over the land instead of the sea, on some local chart of one of the sailors. An instance of how such placing might transfer a name from one coast to the other may be seen in the La Cosa map: of the names relating to Cuba it is impossible to determine to which coast many of them belong (see Fig. 11).

Cabo Santo: Columbus gave the name "Puerto Sancto" to a harbor near the eastern end of Cuba.[39] If this name had been written by some unknown cartographer "P. Santo," it would not be an unlikely change for the Cantino draftsman to interpret "P. Santo" as "Punta Santo" or "Cabo Santo."

Rio de las almadias: This is another descriptive term. Columbus did not give the name to any place on the coast according to any list we have; but, on

---

[39] Journal under date of Dec. 1, 1492 (Raccolta, Part I, Vol. 1, p. 52; Markham, *op. cit.*, p. 93); Las Casas, *op. cit.*, Book I, Ch. 49 (Vol. 1, p. 355).

December 3, he saw five large *almadías*, or canoes.[40]
It may well be that this incident furnished the basis
of the name given to the river.

pũta (Punta) *Roixa:* "The reddish headland." None
of the accounts of the voyage of Columbus gives this
name to any portion of the coast. Under date of
November 25, however, the Journal says[41] that
Columbus found rocks on the shore which seemed to
contain iron and silver. Southern Cuba does contain large deposits of iron. Such an incident would
furnish a sufficient basis to some sailor, in recounting
his experiences on the voyage, to give the name
"Punta Roixa" to the corresponding section of the
coast.

Rio de dõ (don) *diego:* On the La Cosa map the
third name west of the eastern end of Cuba is "R°
de la bega" (Fig. 11). The Cantino map has almost
certainly corrupted this name. The correspondence
seems all the plainer when we point out that in both
cases the name is the third from the eastern end of
Cuba.

C. do fim do abrill: "Cape of the end of April."
On the first voyage Columbus gave the name "Cabo
Alpha et Omega" to the point which he regarded as
the end of the mainland eastward and the first of
the mainland coming west from Cape St. Vincent in

---

[40] Journal under that date (Raccolta, Part I, Vol. 1, p. 53; incomplete
translation in Markham, *op. cit.*, p. 94); Las Casas, *op. cit.*, Book I,
Ch. 49 (Vol. 1, p. 355).

[41] Journal (Raccolta, Part I, Vol. 1, p. 47; Markham, *op. cit.*, p. 85);
Las Casas, *op. cit.*, Book I, Ch. 47 (Vol. 1, p. 346).

Portugal.[42] La Cosa called it Punta de Cuba (Fig. 11). Las Casas tells us that Columbus regarded this cape as the Cape of the land of the Great Khan, i. e. the mainland of Asia. On the second voyage Columbus left the city of Isabella on the northern coast of Española (Haiti) on April 24, 1494, and arrived at the port of San Nicolás at the western extremity of the island on April 29;[43] hence the crossing of the strait between Española and Cuba came on April 30. The name "Cabo do fim do Abrill" seems to have been derived from this fact.

The name must have been communicated to the map-maker by some one not well informed as to the first voyage; but this presents no difficulty, since it is apparent from the study of the names so far considered that the maker of the Cantino map did not have at hand the maps of Columbus and La Cosa nor any of the accounts used by scholars in criticizing the so-called "Florida" of the Cantino map. Harrisse and others, in considering only the written accounts and maps and neglecting the possibility of

[42] Las Casas, *op. cit.*, Book I, Ch. 50 (Vol. 1, p. 360); Ferdinand Columbus, *op. cit.*, Ch. 30, i. e. Ch. 31 (Italian edition, London, 1867, p. 93; English translation in Churchill's Voyages, p. 535); Peter Martyr: De Orbe Novo, First Decade, Book III (translation by MacNutt, *op. cit.*, p. 92); Andrés Bernáldez, *op. cit.*, Seville edition, Vol. 2, p. 41 (also in Raccolta, Part I, Vol. 1, p. 241).

Ferdinand Columbus says the cape was named Cape Alpha and gives no explanation of the meaning of the name. Peter Martyr and Andrés Bernáldez, while explaining the meaning, attribute the name to the second voyage.

[43] Las Casas, *op. cit.*, Book I, Ch. 94 (Vol. 2, p. 51).

oral testimony concerning the discoveries, have failed to take into consideration what was probably the most usual means of communicating the news of the period among the seaport towns of Spain and Portugal. All the names dealt with so far are descriptive terms (derived from events that occurred during the progress of the voyage along the coast of Cuba or from the prominent features of the coast) such as would naturally be communicated orally by a sailor who had taken part in the voyage. Such a person, though himself incapable of making a map of the new discoveries, might be presumed to have described from memory what he had seen. It may well be imagined that, from these accounts, some Portuguese draftsman made rude local charts of the real Cuba. Supposing this chart-maker to have been a man inclined to spell according to sound and capable of omitting a letter occasionally, we may readily visualize the material the Cantino chart-maker used in depicting the northwestern mainland.

These names, picked from descriptions of some two hundred miles of coast (a description covering forty pages in Las Casas' "Historia de las Indias"), would not necessarily mean much were it not that the descriptive terms also correspond in order with the names on the Cantino map. Of the eleven names thought to be derived from the first voyage of Columbus, nine are in the same order in the accounts of Las Casas and others as they are found on the Cantino map. Three, "Canfure," "Costa alta," and "lago luncor," belong to the Rio de Mares region. Four others, "las cabras," "Cabo Santo," "Rio de las almadias," and "Rio de dõ diego," belong to the Puerto Santo region. "C. do fim do abrill" needs no comment on its position. Only two are out of order: "Rio do los largartos" and "pūta Roixa"; the first is an interpolation, the second should be placed between "las cabras" and "Cabo Santo." The coincidence of the meaning and the position of the nine is quite conclusive as to the Columbian source of the names.

It will be noticed that no comment has been made in regard to "Cabo d. licõtir," "Cabo de bõa ventura," "C. delgato," and "cornejo." These names, in part at least, seem to belong to another source than Columbus and their origin will be discussed later.

(B) SOUTHERN COAST

Proceeding in order, we will now consider the southern coast of the Cantino land (Fig. 14). The names here are practically all unidentifiable. They are from east to west: "el golfo bavo," "C. lurcar," "C. do mortinbo," "G. do lurcor," "C. arlear," "Rio do corno," and "Rio de las palmas." On the Canerio map, beyond Rio de las Palmas, there appears one more name than on the Cantino, "lago del lodro" (Fig. 15). This name is near the edge of the Canerio map; it may also originally have been on the Cantino map, and in that case was cut away when the border was trimmed off.

el golfo bavo: This is the first name west of C. do fim do abrill. The first place mentioned by Las Casas and Bernáldez, after Columbus started to coast the island of Cuba on the south on his second voyage, is described by Las Casas[44] as "una gran bahía y puerto grande" named, by Columbus, Puerto Grande. In favor of an identification of "el golfo bavo" with the Puerto Grande there is the fact that in each case the name is the first mentioned west of C. do fim do abrill.

Rio de las palmas: This is another descriptive name such as might have been given almost anywhere on the coast of Cuba. It may be a name transposed from the northern coast, where Columbus on the first voyage gave the name "Cabo de Palmas" to a headland near the point whence he turned back toward Española.[45]

lago del lodro: On the Canerio map only; it seems to belong to the fourth voyage. It is possibly derived from "lugar del oro" or "loco del oro." Veragua was known, from the voyage of 1502, as a land where an abundance of gold was found;[46] in the "Informatione di Bartolomeo Colombo"[47] there is men-

[44] Las Casas, *op. cit.*, Book I, Ch. 94 (Vol. 2, p. 51).

[45] Journal under date of Oct. 30, 1492 (Raccolta, Part I, Vol. 1, p. 32; transl. in Markham, *op. cit.*, p. 63). See also Las Casas, *op. cit.*, Book I, Ch. 44 (Vol. 1, p. 322).

[46] Letter of Columbus of July 7, 1503 (Raccolta. Part I, Vol. 2, p. 198, transl. in R. H. Major, *op. cit.*, p. 197).

[47] (Henry Harrisse:) Bibliotheca Americana Vetustissima: A Description of Works Relating to America Published Between the Years 1492 and 1551, New York, 1866. pp. 471–474. Also in F. R. von Wieser:

tion several times of the abundance of gold. Veragua, as Lochac, was associated in the mind of Columbus with the Golden Chersonese (see the third study, pp. 74–75).

On the Canerio map a grove of trees is shown in the corner of the gulf, with another slightly farther north (Fig. 15). On the Ruysch map of 1508,[48] in the same corner of Asia, there are two groves, one "Silva Ebani" and the other "Silva Aloe." There are other silvae in four places farther south on the same map.

This completes the list of names on the Cantino and Canerio maps which appear to have had their origin in the voyages of Columbus.

NAMES FROM OTHER SOURCES

Some of the names that remain may come from other sources. When it is recalled that Columbus regarded Cuba as the mainland of Asia, it may be worth while to examine the names given to areas which were similarly regarded as Asiatic by one or another map-maker or explorer. There were other such areas in 1500—first, the land discovered by John Cabot and, second, that discovered by the Corte-Reals in 1500.[49] In order to avoid the ques-

Footnote 47, continued

Die Karte des Bartolomeo Colombo über die vierte Reise des Admirals, text and facsimile of three maps, reprint from *Mitt. des Inst. für Österreichische Geschichtsforschung*, Innsbruck, 1893.

[48] Nordenskiöld, Facsimile-Atlas, Pl. 32.

[49] See La Cosa for the Cabot land (Fig. 10; enlarged on Fig. 16), Cantino for the Corte-Real land (Fig. 8).

tion of their identity these two lands may be regarded as distinct; in any case they are represented differently on the charts.

The land discovered by the Cabots[50] is not identifiable, as, apparently, its latitude cannot be determined. Its supposed distance from England was early put in question. The Soncino letter of August 24, 1497,[51] gives it as 400 leagues. This distance was questioned by Ruy Gonzalez de Puebla in his letter to the Catholic sovereigns dated July 25 (?), 1498. Pedro de Ayala, in his despatch of July 25, 1498, says he does not believe that the distance is 400 leagues but that the land was part of what had been discovered for the Spanish sovereigns. The Pasqualigo letter of August 23, 1497, reported Cabot's statement that the distance to the new land was 700 leagues and that it was the mainland of the country of the Great Khan. The second Soncino letter, of December 18, 1497, represents John Cabot as hoping, after occupying the fish country, to "keep on still further towards the East, where he will be opposite to an island called Cipango." Juan de la Cosa delineated the English discoveries along a coast extending east and west (Fig. 10; enlarged on Fig. 16), the most westerly name being apparently considerably

[50] Henry Harrisse: John Cabot, the Discoverer of North America, and Sebastian, His Son, London, 1896, pp. 42–84, 126–141, and 385–469; *idem:* Discovery of North America, pp. 1–50; Charles Deane: The Voyages of the Cabots, in Winsor: Narrative and Critical History, Vol. 3, pp. 1–58.

[51] For this and the following documents see Markham, *op. cit.*, pp. 202, 207, 208–209, 201–202, 203–206.

to the east of the longitude of Española.

Thus it would have been possible for Cabot to continue his voyage westwards " to the East," until he was opposite the island of Cipangu, or the Española of Columbus. No names on this Cabot land can be identified with any of those on the Cantino map.

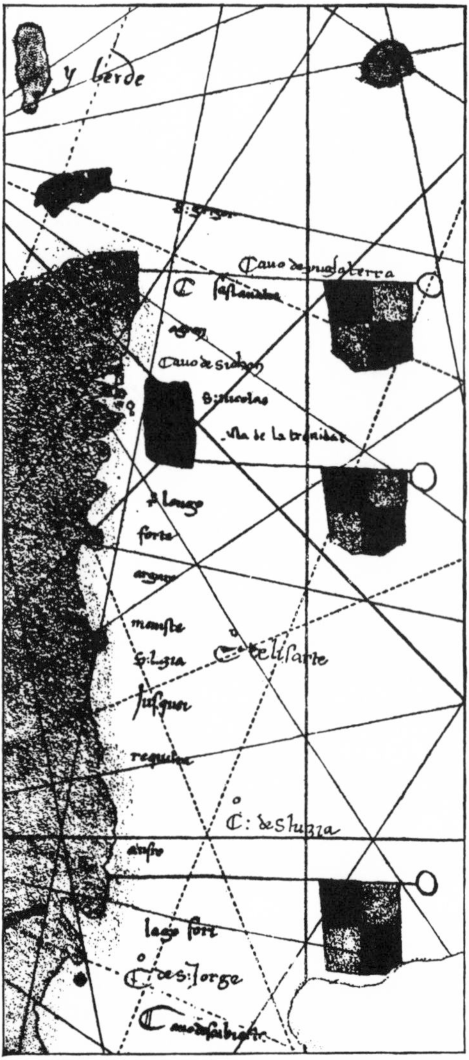

Fig. 16—The land discovered by Cabot, from the La Cosa map (enlarged from the photographic facsimile in Harrisse's Discovery of North America, Pl. 2).

Turning now to the second possibility, four voyages were made by the Portuguese to the northwest in 1500 and following years.[52] Of these, three were made early enough for their results to be incorporated in the Cantino map. Gaspar Corte-Real made the first voyage in 1500 and returned safely. The next year he sailed again, but, while his companion ship reached home, he himself never returned. In 1502 Miguel Corte-Real went to search for his brother with three ships. Arrived on the coast, the ships separated to carry on the search, with the understanding that they would meet again on August 20. Two of the ships kept this rendezvous, but Miguel Corte-Real was never seen again. The land where the Corte-Reals were lost was named "Terra de Corte-Real." Alberto Cantino, in his letter[53] to the Duke of Ferrara, October 17, 1501, reported the distance to the land of Corte-Real as 2800 miles. Pasqualigo, on October 18, 1501, reported the distance as 1800 miles to north and west. The latter also reported that the Portuguese believed this land was joined to the Andilie (the Antilles), discovered by the Spaniards, and to the land of Papagà (Brazil), discovered by Cabral, and that it was the mainland.

On the coast of a peninsula designated "A ponta d' [Asia],"[54] which resembles, and may represent,

[52] Harrisse, Les Corte-Real; *idem:* Découverte ·. . . de Terre-Neuve, pp. 34–50; *idem:* Discovery of North America, pp. 59–76.

[53] For this and the following document see Harrisse, Les Corte-Real, pp. 204–211; also Markham, *op. cit.*, pp. 232–236.

[54] The bracketed word is missing because it was near the border of the map, which was trimmed off. There is no doubt as to the meaning Asia, however, because of the inscription at the side of the peninsula.

Greenland (Fig. 8), the Cantino map contains a legend as follows:[55]

Esta terra he descober[ta] per mandado do muy escelentissimo p[ri]ncepe dom Manuel Rey de portugall aquall se cree ser esta a ponta dasia. E os que a descobriram nam chegarõ a terra mais vironla z nam viram senam serras muyto espessas polla quall segum a opinyom dos cosmofircos se cree ser a ponta dasia. (This land was discovered by order of the very excellent Prince Dom Manoel, King of Portugal, which is believed to be the extremity of Asia. Those who discovered it did not go ashore but saw the land and saw nothing but very serrated mountains; it is for this reason, according to the opinion of cosmographers, that it is believed to be the extremity of Asia.)

The facts rehearsed were a puzzle to cartographers; for they were called upon to delineate a land at once 400 leagues from England, 700 leagues from Bristol, and 1800 or 2800 miles from Lisbon; a land that was the mainland of Asia and that could be coasted westward "to the East" until one was opposite the island of Cipangu; and a land where the Portuguese maps indicated the discoveries of the Corte-Reals on a coast extending north and south so as to join the Andilie land and the land of Papagà.

The cartographer who made the Cantino map put this material together by stripping all the names from the coast of the Terra de Corte-Real, as he had done

---

[55] Stevenson, Maps Illustrating Early Discovery, Portfolio 1. Legend deciphered in Harrisse, Discovery of North America, p. 67.

with the names on the real Cuba, and transferring them, so far as he used them at all, to the supposed mainland of Asia. The land was given the triangular shape indicated in the "Información y testimonio" of Ferdinand Perez de Luna—an eastern coast running many degrees to the north, and a southern coast running, so far as the Cantino map is concerned, to the margin on the west. (This was in conformity with the Behaim-Martellus idea of eastern Asia.) Then, as though not quite certain, he put in the pine-covered land of Terra Corte-Real far to the east on the Portuguese side of the Demarcation Line and somewhat less than half the distance across the ocean from Ireland.

On the eastern and southern coasts of the supposed Asiatic mainland on the Cantino map two names, at least, are found which belong to the Còrte-Real voyages. The second name from the north is *Cabo d. licŏtir* (Fig. 14). Canerio gives the name as "Cabo dellicontir" (Fig. 15). Harrisse suggests[56] that this name is really "Cabo del encontro," or "the cape of the meeting," that is of the meeting appointed by Miguel Corte-Real for August 20, 1502. The other name, *Cabo de bõa ventura*, is the fourth from the north on the Cantino map. This name is Portuguese in form and not Spanish as are the others. A "C[abo] de boa ventura," as well as an "Y[sla] de boa ven-

<hr />

[56] Harrisse, Découverte . . . de Terre-Neuve, p. 359; *idem*, Les Corte-Real, p. 90.

tura," are found on the Pedro Reinel chart, 1505,[57] of the Portuguese possessions. The name "bona ventura" is also found on the Oliveriana chart.[58] After 1520 the name frequently appears on the coast of what finally differentiates itself as Newfoundland.

Still another name that may belong to the Corte-Real voyages is *C. delgato*, or "Cape of the cat." Alberto Cantino, in his letter already cited, refers to ". . . animals, in which the country abounds, such as very large stags with long-haired fur . . .; also wolves, foxes, tigers, and sables" (animali, deli quali el paese abonda, cioè cervi grandissimi vestiti di longissimo pelo . . . ; et cusi lupi, volpe, tigri et zebellini). Harrisse thinks the tiger was the *loup-cervier*, or lynx.[59] In 1505, £5 was paid "to Portyngales that brought popyngais and catts of the mountaigne with other stuf to the Kinge's grace"; or, as elsewhere stated, "wild catts and popyngays of the Newfound Island."[60]   Harrisse expresses doubt about this matter because neither parrots nor catamounts are found in Newfoundland. But popinjays are wood-

[57] Friedrich Kunstmann: Ueber einige der ältesten Karten Amerikas, pp. 125–151 in his "Die Entdeckung Amerikas, nach den ältesten Quellen geschichtlich dargestellt." with an atlas: Atlas zur Entdeckungsgeschichte Amerikas, aus Handschriften der K. Hof- und Staats-Bibliothek, der K. Universität und des Hauptconservatoriums der K. B. Armee herausgegeben von Friedrich Kunstmann, Karl von Spruner, Georg M. Thomas, Royal Bavarian Academy of Sciences, Munich, 1859; reference on Pl. 1 of atlas.

[58] Raccolta, Part IV, Vol. 2, Pl. 2. Also reproduced in Harrisse, Découverte . . . de Terre-Neuve, Pl. 4.

[59] Harrisse, Découverte . . . de Terre-Neuve, p. 45.

[60] Markham, *op. cit.*, p. xxii, note 3; Harrisse, Discovery of North America, p. 47.

peckers as well as parrots.[61]   In general, any gar-
rulous bird might be called a popinjay. The lynx is
often called a catamount, or *gato montés*, by the
Mexicans. The Cabot map of 1544[62] indicates on
the mainland of North America three large animals;
one of these in the east-central region is spotted like
a tiger. The wildcat species is found all over North
America. There is a species, known as the northern
lynx (*Felis canadensis*), whose habitat is the northern
regions, which is thought to be the *loup-cervier* of the
early voyagers; this particular species is not found
south of Pennsylvania. As, however, it is of a uni-
form gray color it does not seem to be the same as that
depicted on the Cabot map and certainly could not
be called a tiger. Another species, called the bay
lynx, or American wildcat (*Felis rufa*), the *gato
montés* of the Mexicans, is found quite generally over
North America as far south as Florida and Mexico.
It is spotted in such a way that it might be called a
tiger and is of such size as to attract immediate attention, being about thirty inches from the tip of the
nose to the root of the tail. Nothing definite can be
asserted about the name "C. delgato" on the basis
of the habitat of the various members of the Felidae.
But the fact that the Portuguese mention tigers in
the north, that the animal is pictured on the Cabot
map, and that there is no mention of Felidae on the

---

[61] See "popinjay" in Webster's Dictionary; also various spellings and
meanings in the Century Dictionary.

[62] Jomard, *op. cit.*, Pl. XX, 1–4; Kretschmer, *op. cit.*, atlas, Pl. 16.
(For further details see third study, p. 84, footnote 52.)

island of Cuba by the early navigators, together with the characteristics of the various wildcats living in the Arctic, temperate, and mountain regions, would all tend to show that the name "C. delgato" belongs to the Portuguese discoveries in the north.

Only one other name on the southern coast of the Cantino map seems to have any relation that can now be determined to the Portuguese explorations to the north. The *C. do mortinbo* may be the same as the "Cavo del Marco," on the southern coast of the Oliveriana map,[63] and the "C. S. Marci" of Johan Ruysch (1508),[64] in the same general position on his Cuba. In any case, its origin is not clear.

Doubtful Names, Some Possibly Derived from the Vespucius Voyage of 1497

Of the names on the Cantino map there remain unidentified and mostly unexplainable in meaning the following: "cornejo," "C. lurcar," "G. do lurcor," "C. arlear," and "Rio do corno."

Some of these names may possibly be derived from the much-disputed Vespucius voyage of 1497, to which reference has already been made (pp. 77-79). Varnhagen and Fiske[65] think he made the voyage in 1497 around the coast of Honduras, Yucatan, the Gulf of Mexico, and Florida to some point on the eastern coast of the present United States. Varn-

[63] See above, footnote 58.

[64] Nordenskiöld, Facsimile-Atlas, Pl. 32.

[65] See references, note 2 above, and, in addition, Fiske, *op. cit.*, Vol. 2, pp. 52–60.

hagen thinks the names on the Cantino continental coast are derived from Vespucius. But, if these names were derived in large part from Columbus and Corte-Real, then the coast was not Florida but Cuba and some part of the northeastern coast of North America. It follows that if Vespucius in 1497 visited the regions mentioned, he sailed along the southern coast of Cuba and not the Gulf coast of the United States. The name "Parias" west of the Gulf on the Waldseemüller map of 1507 seems to be derived from Vespucius.[66] Then in the "Navigatio Prima"[67] Vespucius says "the country was in the torrid zone under the parallel which is called the Tropic of Cancer, where the Pole had an elevation of 23 degrees." This would describe the southern coast of Cuba fairly accurately as shown on the Waldseemüller map of 1507, where the tropic crosses the island of Isabella. Furthermore, the Cantino map has two names, *C. lurcar* and *G. do lurcor* (Fig. 14) which Canerio changes to "Cauo luicar" and "Gorffo do lineor" (Fig. 15). These names may well be "C. linea" and "G. do linea"—"the line" being the tropic. If this be the case, the cartographer of the Cantino map preserved nothing of the voyage of Vespucius except a couple of mutilated names. Even his island of

[66] Shea, in Winsor, Narrative and Critical History, Vol. 2, p. 231.

[67] C. G. Herbermann, edit.: The Cosmographiae Introductio of Martin Waldseemüller in Facsimile, Followed by the Four Voyages of Amerigo Vespucci With Their Translation into English. With an Introduction by Prof. Joseph Fischer, S. J., and Prof. Franz von Wieser, *United States Catholic Hist. Soc. Monogr. 4*, New York, 1907, p. lxvii, translation on p. 122.

Isabella is well north of the tropic; but then it has been shown above that he was trying as best he might to interpret conflicting information. The northward shifting of the Cuban coast was evidently a compromise. The Cabot east-and-west coast was interpreted to be the same mainland as the Cuban coast of the second voyage of Columbus: the one far to the north, the other far to the south, but the Columbus coast more in accord with the theoretical southern coast of Mangi, as shown on the Behaim globe[68] and the Henricus Martellus Germanus[69] map.

One of the main difficulties in accepting the first voyage of Vespucius has been the supposed discovery by him of the mainland before Columbus. That difficulty, however, disappears if his mainland was merely the supposed mainland—the coast of Cuba—and the voyage then becomes little more than a repetition of the first and second voyages of Columbus. In this event, the northwestern navigation of Vespucius was on the northern coast of Cuba, and the Indian raid at the close was somewhere in the Bahama group of islands.

GEOGRAPHICAL THEORIES DETERMINING THE POSITION OF THE CONTINENTAL LAND

It remains to discuss the reason for the great interval on the Cantino map between Española and the C. do fim do abrill, which was filled by the insertion of the island of Isabella.

[68] Ravenstein, *op. cit.*, facsimile of gores of globe.
[69] Nordenskiöld, Periplus, p. 123.

A brief summary is all that need here be given, inasmuch as the relevant geographical conceptions have been discussed in detail in the previous studies. Ptolemy made the known world to extend over approximately 180° from west to east. Marinus of Tyre made this area extend over 225°. Columbus believed, with Marinus of Tyre, that the land from Cape St. Vincent in Portugal to Cattigara at the eastern limit of the known world covered 225° of longitude. The work of the medieval geographers had added to the world as known to the ancients approximately 60°; hence 285° had been accounted for before the voyage of 1492. According to the reckoning of Columbus, counting from the west eastwards, there should be 285° from the first meridian to the extreme point of Asia, the Cabo do fim do abrill, or Cape Alpha et Omega, which would leave 75° from the same starting point westwards to the mainland of Asia. The western end of Española was usually placed between 50° and 60° west of the first meridian; as a consequence, the eastern end of Cuba, being immediately opposite the western end of Española, was between 15° and 25° too far east to represent eastern Asia according to these calculations. When, therefore, a cartographer drew a map of the entire world, the mainland of Asia had to be placed, according to the existing theory, at a greater distance across the Atlantic. What followed was that the Columbian theory was used in plotting the chart westward across the Atlantic; whereas the

Ptolemaic theory was adhered to in delineating the world eastward from the western coast of Europe. This procedure is evident in the Behaim globe, the Waldseemüller map of 1507, and other maps that made the distance from Cape St. Vincent to the eastern side of the Sinus Magnus 180°. Indeed, many of the maps of the early sixteenth century distinctly represent both theories. The Waldseemüller map of 1507 is the first clear example of the whole world so drawn as to embody both theories. The Johan Ruysch map (1508) makes the estimates of Columbus the basis of the map, which Waldseemüller does not quite do. Other cartographers working between 1492 and 1507 avoided the issue by not representing the whole world. La Costa, for instance, omits that portion between Calicut in India and a point west of Cuba, about 140 degrees. It was, apparently, the difficulty of reconciling the Columbian and Ptolemaic theories of geography that led Peter Martyr[70] to say: "It is not without cause that cosmographers have left the boundaries of Ganges India undetermined. There are not wanting those among them who think that the coasts of Spain do not lie very distant from the shores of India."

It is evident, therefore, that Harrisse's argument, that the Cantino continental land could not be Asia because an eastern coast of Asia was already represented, is untenable.

[70] MacNutt, *op. cit.*, Vol. I, p. 92.

CONCLUSION

In conclusion, the present writer is convinced that the continental land northwest of Isabella was not Florida. This land was drawn under the misapprehension that it was the mainland of Asia. The current ideas of eastern Asia, as shown on the Behaim globe and the Henricus Martellus Germanus map, were used, although the gulf was placed a little too far north. We have shown how this was a compromise of the Columbus and Cabot discoveries. The lands actually explored and named under the impression of their being eastern Asia were: Cuba, discovered by Columbus; and the northeastern coast of North America, discovered and explored by John Cabot and the Corte-Reals. The cartographer in endeavoring to digest a mass of conflicting data— theoretical, documentary, cartographical, and oral— produced the result known as the Cantino map.

INDEX

THE TEST OF TIME
by
Clinton R. Edwards
Professor of Geography
The University of Wisconsin-Milwaukee

THE TEST OF TIME

This new edition of George E. Nunn's book is published as part of the American Geographical Society's commemoration of the 500th anniversary of Christopher Columbus' first voyage. The first edition (AGS Research Series, no. 14, 1924) was the Society's most extensive single contribution to Columbiana, although there have been many relevant articles in its scholarly journal, *The Geographical Review*.[1] Impending publication of *Geographical Conceptions* was noted in that journal.[2] The book's importance has been recognized in two reprints.[3]

The work is the published version of Nunn's doctoral dissertation in Social Institutions (sub-field Historical Geography) at the University of California, Berkeley. The original title was "Studies in the Cartography of the New World," and it dealt "with four problems of crucial importance for an understanding of the activities of the discoverer of the New World" (from the graduation brochure). Frederick J. Teggart, to whom *Geographical Conceptions* is dedicated, was chairman of Nunn's doctoral committee and at the time Associate Professor of Sociology. Conferral of the doctorate was in June, 1924.

[1]For bibliography of articles in *Geographical Review* on Columbus and related subjects, see Edwards and Anderson 1992.

[2]"Recent Publications," *The Geographical Review*, v. 14, no. 3, July 1924, pp. 467-468.

[3]Reprints: Freeport, New York: Books for Libraries Press, 1972; New York: Octagon Books, 1977.

The four studies have been regarded as separate subjects by some reviewers and commentators, but they have the common bond of relevance to the overall questions which Nunn considered to be of greatest importance to fifteenth and sixteenth century geography: what was Columbus looking for, and what did he think he found?

None of the four subjects has reached closure among Columbus scholars, so no final judgment of Nunn's contribution can be made. He has been taken to task on particular points, for example by Bigelow (1935), Morison (1941:26; 1991, v.1:60) and Sale (1989:15), but on the other hand many scholars have considered his work valuable and he has often been cited in support of this or that idea or viewpoint.

The early reviews were favorable. "E. H." noted that "He has no novel theories to put forward, but the value of the studies lies rather in the careful sifting of the evidence for and against the views of previous writers, and the selection of such conclusions as seem to bear the test of critical examination." ("E. H." 1925:465-466). John Bigelow, who later was to disagree with Nunn's interpretation of the "Bartholomew Columbus maplets," did not accept Nunn's methods or conclusions on all points, but his review was also generally favorable (Bigelow 1925:601-603).

This essay is not intended to be another review of, or an introduction to, *Geographical Conceptions*. Nor is its objective a final judgment concerning the validity of Nunn's conclusions. Rather, it is an attempt to trace the course of his arguments in his own later contributions and in the hands of other scholars, and to determine to what extent we are closer to answers, building upon his work. Since the essay deals with the subsequent explication of the various theses presented by Nunn, I recommend that his text be read first.

"The Determination of the Length of a Terrestrial Degree by Columbus"

Much of Nunn's commentary on Columbus' motives and rationale for his "Enterprise of the Indies" hinges upon his use of a short estimate for the length of a meridional degree or degree of longitude at the equator. Despite learned opinions and the usage of contemporary Portuguese navigators (usually 66²/₃ miles per degree), Columbus insisted that the correct measure was a much shorter 56²/₃ miles. Nunn assumed these to be "Roman" or "Italian" miles of 1,480 meters. Along with the exaggerated eastward extension of continental Asia, this made for a relatively short oceanic distance between Spain and Japan or China. Columbus claimed to have checked this measure on voyages between Lisbon and the Guinea Coast. In this chapter, Nunn reacted to Vignaud's criticism that Columbus did not possess the expertise to make an empirical test of the measure (pp. 2-5).

The elements of Nunn's explication of how Columbus could have checked the measure he found in literature are: the length of an "Italian nautical mile," 1,480 meters; the erroneous latitudes of Lisbon and "Los Idolos" (modern Isles de Los, off Conakry, Republic of

Guinea) as available to Columbus; the modern measure of a mean meridional degree; and the distance between Lisbon and Los Idolos and their geographical positions as taken from a modern chart (pp. 13-18).

These elements included some assumptions and some errors. Perhaps the weakest assumption was that Portuguese pilots had determined accurately the distance involved, and thus the modern distance was acceptable in the calculation. Also, the determination of the "Italian mile" of Columbus at 1,480 meters is not accepted universally.

Nunn erred slightly in using the "accepted value of 111,121 meters for a mean meridional degree." That is close to the mean figure for degrees from the Equator to one of the Poles, but closer to the mark for his calculation would have been the mean figure for the degrees between Lisbon and Los Idolos, about 110,796 meters. However, this makes but a negligible difference in the calculation.

The most serious discrepancy lies in Nunn's interpretation of the latitude of Los Idolos as stated by Columbus. The assumption for Lisbon is based reasonably on the latitude as shown on contemporary charts. But the latitude for Los Idolos as given by Columbus is subject to variant translations. Nunn chose the one ($1°$ 05' N.) that results in the figure closest to $56\frac{2}{3}$ miles for the length of a meridional degree.

We can do little to refine the first assumption, since there is no consensus on precisely how long Columbus' nautical miles were. Charlier (1987) concluded that they were the "Roman mile of about 1,480 meters," but Kelley suggested that the measure was 4,060 English feet or 1,238 meters. Later he changed his estimate to about 4,100 feet or 1,250 meters as necessary to fit the two legs of Columbus' first voyage. However, he used the former figure to represent the geometric mile of portolan charts in his simulation of the first voyage (Kelley 1983:91, 102-104; 1987:122-123). If substituted in Nunn's calculation, this figure brings the measure of a degree closer to that used by the Portuguese, but since other elements of Nunn's calculations can be questioned, this does not aid analysis.

Nunn's latitude difference between Lisbon and Los Idolos, inferred as available to Columbus, was 39° 10′ (p. 17). This was based on his translation of Columbus' commentary on José Vizinho's observation: *invenit se distare ab equinoxiali gradus .v. minute in insula vocata de los Ydolos* (Postille 1892-96:369) as " . . . he found that he was distant from the equator one degree five minutes on an island called 'Los Ydolos' . . . " (p. 6). Nunn developed the theory that with these data Columbus could have checked empirically the length of a degree, and due to fortuitous errors in the data the result was about $56^{2}/_{3}$ Roman miles, which matched what he had found in literature.

Nunn reiterated in subsequent monographs and articles that Columbus claimed he had more than a literary basis for his measure of a degree (Nunn 1928:4; 1932:15-17). This became important to his further discussions of Columbus' concepts of the longitudinal spacing of various parts of the world, of Columbus' motives, and his interpretations of where he had been and what he had discovered. Later, Nunn placed even more emphasis on the claim of empirical verification, concluding that Columbus did not obtain his figure of 56$\frac{2}{3}$ miles from D'Ailly's *Imago Mundi*. He reiterated his calculations in *Geographical Conceptions*, retaining the latitude of 1° 05′ for Los Idolos (Nunn 1935:656).

As his interest in Columbus' geographical conceptions continued, Nunn depended even more heavily on the 56$\frac{2}{3}$ mile degree in explaining Columbus' view of the earth and its consequences for his actions. He noted the difference between "the current European belief that an equatorial degree of Ptolemy's was equal to 62$\frac{1}{2}$ Italian miles" and the Columbus degree of 56$\frac{2}{3}$ miles. Still apparently chastising Vignaud, he wrote: "Modern critics avoid the consequences of this discrepancy by denying that Columbus made a verification of the 56$\frac{2}{3}$ mile measure" (Nunn 1937:28).

It was inevitable that someone would prefer a different translation of Columbus' postil. In 1928 Alberto Magnaghi stated that Columbus intended five degrees and some or a few minutes for the latitude of Los Idolos (Magnaghi 1928:467). Despite this, Nunn reiterated his demonstration that it "actually was possible for Columbus to assemble data that could have convinced him that he had confirmed the Arabian estimate of 56$\frac{2}{3}$ miles for an equatorial degree." He retained his original translation of the latitude of Los Idolos, "1° 5′ N. Lat." (Nunn 1937:29).

Morison's version of the Latin was "*g. V. minute*," as he saw in the original. He agreed with Magnaghi's translation and wrote it as "5 degrees (gradus) and some minutes." After pointing out what in his view was Nunn's mistranslation, he offered his proofs ("There is really no room for argument . . . ") that Columbus indeed intended about 5° for the latitude of Los Idolos. Morison reiterated that Nunn "had translated this postil wrong." He added that Columbus' belief that Portuguese pilots could estimate distances and measure latitudes accurately was "simply ludicrous," thus destroying in his mind one of the major underpinnings of Nunn's argument. Morison was so adamant on this point that he denied the contemporary Portuguese the ability to determine latitude, even roughly, by noon sun sight. This was on the grounds that "they had not yet learned the trick of taking a meridional altitude of the sun and applying declination to find latitude." As proof he pointed out that even the expert Vizinho could not determine correctly the latitude of Los Idolos (Morison 1941:26n; 1991 v.1:54-55). Whether or not Vizinho could do so depends on the interpretation of Columbus' postil recording the event. Commentary on E. G. R. Taylor's interpretation, which absolves Vizinho of error, is given below.

Laguarda also translated Columbus' Los Idolos latitude as "*5° y minutos*," and later expressed the opinion that Columbus could not have determined empirically that a degree at the Equator contained 56²/₃ miles (Laguarda 1963:199; 1974:37).

Consuelo Varela was equivocal on this point; her transcription of the postil was *"gradus V minute,"* which she translated as *"5 grados y minutos."* However, in a footnote she wrote, *"Quizá se deba traducir: 'un grado y cinco minutos.' La latitud en todo caso es errónea"* ("Perhaps it should be translated: 'One degree and five minutes.' In any case the latitude is wrong") (Varela 1984:11).

Most recently, Randles, citing Magnaghi and Laguarda, wrote: "Nunn's demonstration of how Columbus had performed the verification of the figure [56²/₃ miles for a meridional degree] is vitiated by his misreading of the latitude of the Los Idolos islands referred to in one of Columbus' notes: '1° 5' N', instead of '5° . . . minutes N.' " (Randles 1990:64n).

Thus the weight of opinion and Morison's arguments favored translation as "5° [and a few] minutes." This brings Columbus' version of José Vizinho's observation considerably closer to the mark, but still in surprisingly large error for an expert. The actual latitude of Los Idolos is 9° 30' N.

E. G. R. Taylor presented an intriguing variant interpretation of Columbus' postil. Her translation was: " . . . he found that he was 5 minutes of a degree from the equinoctial, in the island called Los Idolos . . . " However, Taylor pointed out that the observation was made on land, and thus could not have been so inaccurate—more than 9° off. Also, it was made on the day of the spring equinox. For her, " . . . the figure recorded in the note ["*g. V. minute*"] was that of the solar declination, not the distance of the island from the equator." She adds that "The Admiral's Latin was notoriously ungrammatical" (Taylor 1952:51). Acceptance of her suggestion might be furthered by translation of the phrase as " . . . he found it [the sun] distant from the Equator 5 minutes," but a Latin grammarian might not agree.

We may never know what Columbus meant by this figure. The consequences for Nunn's calculation are obvious: it works only by use of the translation considered least likely by the other scholars cited.

Starting with Vignaud, the discussion comes full circle with Harley's judgment: "The consensus is that [Columbus] lacked instruments precise enough to accomplish this [the empirical verification of the length of a meridional degree]. The likelihood is that he was merely confirming what he hoped to find" (Harley 1990:42). Morison had come to a similar conclusion: "Columbus obviously fudged his figures to fit a preconceived length of the degree" (Morison 1991 v.1:79-80, 82).

All of this does not change the fact that Columbus believed in and used a measure of $56^2/3$ miles for the length of an equatorial degree of longitude or a meridional degree. This was a basic element in Nunn's arguments concerning Columbus' views of the world and oceanic distances. But it does cast serious doubt on Nunn's claim that Columbus could have verified the measure empirically while voyaging between Lisbon and Guinea, and on Columbus' claim that he did so.

"THE ROUTE OF COLUMBUS ON HIS FIRST VOYAGE AS EVIDENCE OF HIS KNOWLEDGE OF THE WINDS AND CURRENTS OF THE ATLANTIC"

As with the first chapter, Nunn begins this one by disagreeing with Vignaud (pp. 31-33). In 1492 Columbus sailed approximately along the latitude of the Canary Islands, not, as Vignaud claimed, because of foreknowledge of lands to the west or following the directions of an "unknown pilot," but because of his "scientific preparation" for the first voyage. This partly underlay Nunn's reasoning about Columbus' insistence on the nearness of eastern Asia to Europe, discussed in the first chapter, and his study of "the problem of navigating the Atlantic" in this one.

Nunn did not claim categorically that Columbus had complete foreknowledge of the wind and current patterns of the North Atlantic from observations during his voyaging to Atlantic islands and the Guinea Coast. However, he obviously thought that enough knowledge was available to Columbus before the first voyage to enable him to figure out the best routes going and returning. An element missing from Nunn's discourse is the considerable doubt as to precisely where Columbus traveled during his pre-1492 "Portuguese years," the number of times he voyaged to Guinea (most likely only once), and whether or not he visited the Azores and Iceland. His "key points" from which Columbus would have had the opportunity to gain knowledge of the Atlantic were the Canaries, Madeiras, and Azores.

There is no doubt that Columbus visited the Canaries and Madeiras, but I have found no sure statement about the Azores. Morison, who treated Columbus' pre-1492 voyaging in the greatest detail, was indefinite on this point: " . . . on Corvo there was a natural rock statue of a horseman pointing westward. Columbus is said to have seen this on one of his early voyages . . . " No source was cited, and Morison did not otherwise place Columbus at the Azores before 1493. He did note that "More substantial evidence of exotic lands to the westward was collected by Columbus during his residence in Portugal and the islands" (*i.e.*, in the Atlantic islands generally, including the Canaries and Madeiras), but the Azores were not specified (Morison 1991 v.1:79-80, 82).

Without citation of source, Taviani had Columbus sailing to the Azores before 1492, but on the same page he revealed that support for the allegation is weak: "The knowledge he demonstrated in the waters of the Azores during the voyages of the grand discovery gives us assurance that he had also navigated among these islands during his Portuguese period" (Taviani 1991:39). However, these doubts do not eliminate the islands from Nunn's thesis; Columbus could have learned, and according to his son Ferdinand did learn, much about Azorean waters from Portuguese sailors.

Without citing Nunn, Captain Menander in 1926 disagreed with his general proposition, inferring that from a sailor's viewpoint there was no way that knowledge of conditions near Old World shores could yield knowledge of atmospheric or oceanic circulation patterns in the farther reaches of the Atlantic (Menander 1926:665).

Having read *Geographical Conceptions*, Lieutenant McElroy, Morison's co-investigator of Columbus' navigation, wrote: "The eastward and westward sailing tracks selected by Columbus were in my opinion not based upon scientific observation or secret knowledge, but were a combination of good fortune, better judgment, and the best traditions of navigation" (McElroy 1941:212).

Not surprisingly, Morison's comment was consistent with McElroy's: "There is no hint in the Journal [the *diario* of the first voyage] or elsewhere that Columbus knew that the northeast trade wind would carry him across; but he must have observed on his African voyage that a westward course from the Canaries would enjoy a fair wind as soon as you pass out of the Canary calms. It was merely his good fortune that the same wind carried his fleet all the way to America" (Morison 1941:207).

The opposite view was taken by Taviani, who followed Nunn closely: "Porto Santo [Madeiras], the Canaries, and the Azores were three points in a geographic and maritime equation whose solution granted mastery of the Atlantic. With the marine sense that distinguished him, Columbus found that solution between 1476 and 1484 . . . " Further, if this were not true, " . . . it would be hard to explain why Columbus left Palos, headed straight for the Canaries, and from there confidently sailed west. Likewise it would be hard to explain why, on his return, he displayed not the least hesitation in sailing north to the latitude of the Azores . . . " (Taviani 1991:38-41).

There is, of course, another explanation. Elaboration of the thesis suggested by Menander and McElroy supplies perhaps the simplest one: that on the outbound voyage Columbus utilized latitude sailing to reach his first objective. His claim to have studied available maps and charts which depicted *Cipango* (Japan) allows the assumption that he sailed to the Canaries so as to reach the latitude of *Cipango*, then sailed westward on that parallel. This had the added attraction of allowing last-minute provisioning and final preparation of the vessels before the long crossing. There may also have been political reasons for this choice (Ramos 1988).

Likewise, explanation of the homeward route does not require foreknowledge of the wind and current patterns. The choice was not up to Columbus. In the face of easterly tradewinds, and knowing that his objective was north rather than south of his starting point, he could only choose the starboard tack (with the wind blowing over his starboard side), which forced a northerly course. The port tack would have diverged much farther from the direct course to Spain. Except for some tacking in variable winds, he held the northerly course to pick up the latitude of the Azores, which he knew, and encountered favorable winds before he reached that latitude. Several storms interfered with his following the appropriate parallel in to Palos.

If this view is accepted, McElroy's comment seems particularly apropos: "Although Columbus has been credited with sailing a 'scientific' course back to Spain, it is evident from his belief that he could sail a straight course that he knew little of the trades and nothing of the northern westerlies. How could he?" (McElroy 1941:227).

The question of Columbus' foreknowledge took on a new flavor with the suggestion by Ramos that the routes of the various voyages were determined partly by experiment and the wish to explore for additional islands. The early part of the first voyage return is explained by the wish to find more new lands to the east of Española. In subsequent voyaging, Columbus wanted to establish and dominate the most efficient routes for commercial advantage (Ramos 1988). This experimentation almost led to disaster on the second voyage return, a lengthy passage so delayed by adverse tradewinds that food and water were almost gone when port was finally made at Cadiz.

Ramos's careful analysis of the *diario* and other evidence has set the pattern for future attempts to determine the real rationale for the routes. He showed that the questions are more complex than merely determining whether or not Columbus had foreknowledge of wind and current patterns.

"DID COLUMBUS BELIEVE THAT HE
REACHED ASIA ON HIS FOURTH VOYAGE?"

Nunn's next joust was with scholars who "have adopted the view that it had dawned upon Columbus, before his death, that he had discovered a new world distinct from the India and Cathay which had been the original object of his search." Much of the subsequent commentary revolved around his acceptance that Columbus' objectives were indeed India and Cathay, and that he died believing that he had reached the outskirts of Asia. Japan as an original objective was largely bypassed in Nunn's discussion. Another important conclusion was that on the fourth voyage Columbus sought a strait by which to pass from the east coast of Asia (Central America) to the neighborhood of the Ganges and India.

Nunn's approach once more was to see whether cartographical evidence could shed light on the subject. The stated elements of his argument were the " . . . three Bartholomew Columbus sketch maps (ca. 1503) . . . the Behaim globe and the map of Juan de la Cosa. With these materials [presumably including the literature listed on p. 57] we may proceed to reconstruct the Columbian geography of 1502."

It is well accepted that in its portrayal of east Asia the Behaim globe reflects Ptolemy's and Marco Polo's geographies, and that Juan de la Cosa's portrayal of the New World was based largely on personal observation or direct testimony of pilots, plus indistinct knowledge of John Cabot's discovery in the northeast.

Columbus scholars are well aware of the continuing commentary on the relationship of the Behaim globe to contemporary maps, particularly those produced by Martellus, ca. 1490. Attempts have been made to associate the globe and these maps directly with Columbus (Davies 1977), but in the main the evidence derives circumstantially from resemblances between them and inference based on the whereabouts of the principals at various times.

Commentary, indeed much disagreement, continues concerning the state of the Juan de la Cosa map, ranging from acceptance of the date on the map to opinions that it was redrawn or modified as much as eight or ten years later. Nunn took the latter view, concluding that it is a copy made about 1508 and revised significantly after 1500 (Nunn 1934).

Further commentary on Martin Behaim and Juan de la Cosa would occupy much more than the pages available to me. More critical to Nunn's argument were the "Bartholomew sketch maps" (hereinafter referred to as the "maplets"), and it is their use for which Nunn has been criticized most effectively.

Nunn's initial knowledge of the maplets was from Fr. R. von Wieser's article in 1893 recording his "discovery" of the manuscript containing them (Wieser 1893). Their existence had been made known earlier (Bigelow 1935:655 notes a citation in 1866), but Wieser was the first to offer analysis and commentary. The reproductions by Wieser are accurate hand-drawn facsimiles, and these are the versions reproduced by Nunn in *Geographical Conceptions*. The originals were drawn in the margins of a manuscript translation to Italian (Zorzi n.d.) of the Columbus letter of July 7, 1503 from Jamaica (the *"Lettera Rarissima,"* hereinafter referred to as *"Lettera"*). This was sufficient for Nunn to attach great importance to the maplets as witness to Columbus' geographical conceptions, especially those resulting from the fourth voyage. Thus far, he had relied on Wieser's commentary, which omitted a number of important points about the provenance and placement of the maplets in the manuscript. Moreover, Wieser's analysis fell short of full explication of just how they appeared on the margins of the manuscript pages.

By 1928 Nunn had become deeply interested in questions surrounding " . . . the greatest problem of early Sixteenth Century geography—the geographical relation of the Trans-Atlantic discoveries to the lands of eastern Asia" (Nunn 1928:2). Crucial to solution were the maplets. Referring to them as "the map of 1506 attributed to Bartholomew Columbus," they would " . . . clear up some of the difficulties of the early Sixteenth Century geography." By the use of "attributed" he seems to have been aware of some pitfalls in uncritical acceptance of Bartholomew's authorship. However, he forged ahead: "This map, small and rude as it is and little advertised as it is, is nevertheless probably the most important map historically ever drawn" (Nunn 1928:8). He again reproduced Wieser's facsimiles of the maplets and wove them intricately with other maps into his portrayal of Columbus' world after the fourth voyage.

The burden of Nunn's 1928 monograph was the role of Francesco Roselli's maps in showing the geographical conceptions of Columbus. Although they and the maplets were used by Nunn to support his views, he did not dwell on any possible direct relationship between features or place names on the two sets of maps as far as origins are concerned. He did suggest that "Roselli used the map or letter of Bartholomew Columbus or information derived therefrom . . . " (Nunn 1928:20). But he did not pursue the point beyond stating that the occurrence of Columbus place names on the "Roselli B" map [the oval mappamundi] " . . . establishes this map as one of the most important records left to us of the fourth voyage of Columbus. It ranks next in importance to the map of Bartholomew Columbus and the letters of the Admiral" (Nunn 1928:20).

The matter of relationships between the maplets and two of Roselli's mappaemundi will be elaborated presently; for the moment, we continue along the trail of the maplets themselves.

Serious criticism of Wieser's interpretations of the maplets, and by implication Nunn's, appeared about a decade after publication of *Geographical Conceptions*, in an article by John Bigelow (1935). After disagreeing with Wieser on several points concerning the origin of a prototype for the maplets, he characterized as "unproved" the notion that Columbus' objective on the first voyage was to find a route to China or India by sailing west, and the notion that the object of the "coastwise cruise" of the fourth voyage was to find a passage to the Indian Ocean. For Bigelow, Columbus' major objective was to find gold, or unclaimed land that he could exploit.

Bigelow then proceeded to discussion of the maplets. The originals appear in the manuscript of a planned work on voyages and travels or new European discoveries by Alessandro Zorzi. Apparently started during the first decade of the sixteenth century, it was never published, and the extant manuscript is a draft with a number of glosses and corrections. It contains an Italian translation of Christopher's *Lettera*, with the maplets drawn at the bottoms of three pages. Bigelow demonstrated the rather inept handling by Wieser of data concerning the maplets' origins and other points. He objected particularly to Wieser's claim that they replicate a lost Columbus map given to Zorzi by Bartholomew. The arguments are involved, indeed convoluted. Bigelow's conclusions that pertain directly to Nunn were that the maplets are not "an exposition of Columbian geography between 1503 and 1506," but demonstrate "the geographical notions of Alessandro Zorzi about twenty years later, some of them derived from the Columbus brothers" (Bigelow 1935:656). Nunn had treated the maplets as a single world map, but Bigelow considered them two separate maps, Nunn's Figures 6 and 7 as one, and Figure 5 as the other. Bigelow reproduced photographically the maplets as they appear in the Zorzi manuscript, at the bottom margins of pages containing the translation of the *Lettera*.

Although Bigelow's analysis and criticisms were directed at Wieser's work, if accepted they destroy Nunn's thesis of the maplets as reflecting directly the Columbus concept of the world after the fourth voyage. In his survey in 1939 of "recent literature and present opinion" on Columbus, Nowell commented that Bigelow "raises some objections to this map [the maplets] as a guide to Columbus geography, holding that the version we have is a revision made by one Alessandro Zorzi some twenty years later. No great attention seems to have been paid to Bigelow's contention" (Nowell 1939:818). As we shall see presently, perhaps closer heed should have been paid to Bigelow's reservations.

Nunn did not respond immediately in print. Two years after Bigelow's article appeared, Nunn continued his analysis of sources for the Columbus concepts, and continued his use of "the maplets attributed to Bartholomew Columbus" in elaborating further the relationship between the Columbian view of the world and the degree of 56$\frac{2}{3}$ miles (Nunn 1937). A major point in this discussion was a legend on one of the maplets (Nunn's Fig. 7) which he assumed derived from Columbus. The legend, spanning the Equator at the western edge of the maplet, notes varying interpretations of the distance between Cabo San Vicente (Portugal) and Cattigara, a place in Southeast Asia near the eastern edge of the "known world." Nunn's transcription is "*Socõdo Marino e Col° da .c. sã Vicẽtio a Cathicara .g. 225. sia* [*sic*, for *sõ*]

hore .15. Secōdo Ptol. in fino a Cattigara .g. 180. che sia
hore 12." His translation is "According to Marinus (of
Tyre) and Columbus from Cape San Vicente (in
Portugal) to Cattigara there are 225 degrees which are
equivalent to 15 hours. According to Ptolemy to the
extremity (of the known world) at Cattigara there are
180° which are equivalent to 12 hours" (Nunn 1937:28).
The longitude is much exaggerated by the figure (225°)
identified in the legend with Columbus. This was a
critical point in Nunn's argument.

He also continued his series of disagreements with
Vignaud, becoming somewhat more vehement: "Henry
Vignaud's viewpoint in regard to the influence of
Marinus of Tyre on Columbus is untenable. Moreover
his thesis, in regard to longitudes, is false" (Nunn
1937:31). Nunn reiterated a major conclusion based on
the maplets: "[They] make two changes in the previous
concepts [*i.e.*, those of Columbus] concerning South
American geography in order to conform to the newly
discovered facts. South America — El Nuevo Mundo — is
itself made into an Asiatic peninsula, and Cattigara is
placed on its west coast."

Nunn did not ignore Bigelow. In a footnote relevant to
his use of one of the maplets to make a significant point,
he wrote: "John Bigelow has written an article on these
Bartholomew Columbus maplets. The writer reserves
comment on this article for another time" (Nunn
1937:35).

In 1936 Roberto Almagià published a thorough
analysis of the provenance of the maplets and some

similar sketches that appear in another of Zorzi's manuscripts. He made reference to *Geographical Conceptions* and had nearly finished his work when Bigelow's article appeared. He incorporated comment on the latter's conclusions and agreed that Wieser was incorrect in attributing the maplets directly to Bartholomew (Almagià 1936).

It was not until after writing at least two intervening articles on other subjects that Nunn faced Bigelow's and Almagià's criticisms. In 1952 he published what was to be his last word on the maplets, going into the matter of their provenance much more deeply than he had in 1924 (Nunn 1952). He included photocopies of the maplets rather than Wieser's facsimiles, but like Wieser he blanked out the text of the *Lettera*.

Nunn accepted "to a certain point the joint theses of Bigelow and Almagià." He conceded that the maplets were not entirely the work of Bartholomew, and blamed Wieser for misrepresenting them as true facsimiles and accepting them as an entire world map showing the explorations of the fourth voyage. But he insisted that the maplets are indeed one map, not two, and reiterated that they "are an interpretation of the Columbus brothers' concept of world geography." He accepted that Zorzi drew the maplets, proved by the fact that they include two different representations of the east coast of Asia (in Figures 5 and 6). The Columbus brothers would not have provided such conflicting views after the fourth voyage. However, the western part of Figure 5 could only have been drawn with " . . . direct evidence from

Bartholomew . . . " There is much other discussion and defense of his conclusions about the maplets and other evidence of Columbus' view of the world. The most interesting point favoring the conclusion that at least the Asian-Central American part of Figure 5 derived from Bartholomew is Nunn's suggestion that this part was mistakenly rotated ninety degrees clockwise by Zorzi. To support this he invoked similar disorientations elsewhere in Zorzi's work. As Nunn illustrated, if rotated back, this part conforms remarkably with the modern map of Central America from the Bay Islands to Panama (Nunn 1952:13).

Nunn stopped short of conceding that the maplets, with the exception of the Asian-Central American part of Figure 5, were conceived as well as drawn by Zorzi, not Bartholomew. His last word was, "With the exception of the geography of the north shore of the Caribbean [referring to the misplacement of the Greater Antilles], these maps are better evidence in their exposition of the Columbus thesis that the transatlantic discoveries constituted a part of Asia than any other [contemporary] cartographic work now known . . . " (Nunn 1952:22).

The latest word on the maplets was by Sale: "It is perhaps worth noting, G. E. Nunn to the contrary [citing Nunn, 1932], that the famous 'maplets' of Bartolomé Colón, Cristóbal's brother, not only do not show the Admiral's ideas of the world at the time of his death but are not even by Bartolomé. On these scruffy pages, perhaps done by Alessandro Zorzi himself, the southern continent is pictured as part of the mass of

Asia, but the entire geography is so erroneous—the islands of the Indies are in completely the wrong places, there is no Cuba or Cipango, the equator is misdrawn, etc.— that we can be quite sure they did not represent Bartolomé's ideas, much less the Admiral's" (Sale 1989:15).

This complete rejection requires further comment; the truth of the matter lies somewhere among Nunn's, Bigelow's and Sale's views.

As noted, the maplets were drawn in the margins of Zorzi's manuscript translation of the *Lettera*. For convenience I shall continue to use, and refer to them as, Nunn's Figures 5, 6 and 7 in *Geographical Conceptions*, copies of Wieser's carefully hand-drawn facsimiles. Although separated from the writing, they do not differ materially from the originals.[4] Figures 6 and 7 are on opposite pages (fols. 56v and 57r) of the *Lettera*, whereas Figure 5 is by itself on fol. 60v. The juxtaposition of Figures 6 and 7 led Bigelow to regard them as one map, showing the world continuously from the Atlantic eastward to eastern Asia. This is supported by internal evidence—the continuous Equator, with each ten degrees numbered, the fit of East Africa, and the legend concerning longitude which refers to the whole extent of the world between Cape St. Vincent and Cattigara. That Figure 5 was intended as a separate map is indicated by the lack of numbers along the graduated

[4]In 1952 Nunn published photocopies of the maplets, separating them from the text of the *Lettera*. On the Africa map he wiped out the symbol and toponym for São Jorge da Mina on the Guinea coast, and neglected to excise part of a text word, "-cano" in "navicano" just east of Gades (Cadiz).

Equator, the different shape of Africa, and especially the very different shape of eastern Asia, at the left.

The crucial point for Nunn's arguments and Sale's refutation is the origin of the data shown on these maplets. They appear with the *Lettera* because of their relevance to Columbus' text. There seems no question that all three were drawn by Zorzi, but how did he get the information?

At this point we introduce a document which has received little attention as providing additional perspective and information on the fourth voyage. It is Zorzi's version of the *Informatione* of Bartholomew (Zorzi 1504?), paraphrased and edited heavily to the extent of turning around the direction in which events and descriptions occurred. It appears in the same collection of papers as the *Lettera*. The narrative starts in Panama and ends with the ships heading from the Bay Islands of Honduras toward Cuba and Española. Zorzi omits whatever may have been said about the marooning at Jamaica and subsequent events, referring his readers to the *Lettera*.

The *Informatione* yields insight into its origin and perhaps that of the maplets. There has been some confusion as to just how the document got into Zorzi's hands. Some authors have presumed that he received it and a map directly from Bartholomew, while others mention an intermediary, a priest in Rome. The only evidence is in the document itself, which has the following account, here summarized.

Shortly after Christopher's death in May, 1506,

Bartholomew went to Rome to enlist the Pope's support for another voyage to Veragua. He brought along a "*disegnio*" (map?) and his description of lands and people encountered on the fourth voyage, perhaps written in 1504 (At the end of the title is a date, "15 [illegible] 4"). Zorzi dates Bartholomew's arrival in 1505, which is not consistent with his statement that Bartholomew arrived after Christopher's death. At any rate, Bartholomew gave his document and *disegnio* to his confessor, a priest named Jerome, of St. John Lateran in Rome. At some unspecified later time, Brother Jerome met Zorzi in Venice and gave him the *disegnio* and the document that was to become the *Informatione*. As noted above, Zorzi included in his drafts his version of the document, "*li quali in brieve Io Alex°* [illegible] *li noterò . . .* " (which I, Alex . . . note down in brief).

The *Informatione*, like the *Lettera*, is interleaved with manuscript and printed pages of Zorzi's projected edition of voyages, travels and new discoveries. Bigelow attached some significance to the order in which various elements—the *Informatione*, the *Lettera*, the maplets—now appear in this assemblage. He concluded that the maplets contained "the geographical notions of Alessandro Zorzi about twenty years later [than the period 1503-1506], some of them derived from the Columbus brothers." Then, rather curiously, he denied that a separate description, which became the *Informatione*, was transmitted by Brother Jerome to Zorzi along with a map (Bigelow 1935:656). But if not, how did Zorzi come by the information, and why did he attribute it to Bartholomew? I see no cogent reason for denying that the information came from the document conveyed by Bartholomew via Brother Jerome.

At this point we return to the concomitant question, how did Zorzi get the information for the maplets other than from Bartholomew? Nunn seems to have been close to an answer when he wrote about the Roselli maps, but he stopped short of associating them directly with the maplets (Nunn 1928). At that time he had not delved more deeply into the matter of provenance.

Nunn noted that the Roselli maps "are a record of Columbus' fourth voyage . . . " The first is the "Contarini-Roselli," the earliest known printed map to portray the new discoveries, dated 1506. It has no Columbus place names, but off the coast of east Asia a legend records Columbus' voyaging. The "oval mappamundi" and the "portolan," undated but probably drawn between 1506 and 1508,[5] contain toponyms assigned to Central American places during the fourth voyage. It seems fairly safe to assume that some of these derived from the *Lettera*, which had been published in Italian before the maps were printed. At least no other source is readily apparent. However, not all of the Columbus names on the Roselli maps occur in the *Lettera*. The names attached to the Bay Islands occur elsewhere at this time only in the *Informatione* and on two of the maplets (Figures 5 and 6). As far as can be determined, the *Informatione* was not published

[5]Almagià, 1951, pp. 33-34, suggests 1508 for these maps. For reproductions see Nebenzahl, 1990, p. 47 for Contarini-Roselli, and p. 56-57 for the Roselli portolan and oval mappaemundi.

until Harrisse's transcription in 1866 (Harrisse 1866:471-474). Thus, circumstantially, Roselli must have obtained the Bay Island place names from Zorzi. He could have obtained the other toponyms from either the *Lettera* or Zorzi. Whatever the case, it seems quite probable that the east Asian parts of the Roselli maps and the Zorzi maplets contain information Bartholomew brought to Rome.

A remaining question is how Zorzi obtained the version of the *Lettera* he wrote in Italian and illustrated with the maplets. The printed translation to Italian was published May 7, 1505, in Venice (Thacher 1903-4 v. 2: 682). The simplest hypothesis is that Zorzi copied this version into his notes and added the maplets.

The east coast of Asia in Figure 6 is similar to its portrayal on the Roselli maps. This suggests that for drawing this maplet Zorzi combined the data from a map by Bartholomew and/or the *Informatione* with the coastal outline of a Roselli map. There is a puzzle here; if at this point Zorzi had both a Bartholomew map and the *Informatione*, why do the place names but not the more correct outline of Central America in Figure 5 occur on the Roselli maps?

Presumably, Zorzi altered the concept of the east coast of Asia on Figure 5 according to Bartholomew's information. There is no indication in the *Informatione* (or the *Lettera*) of how the coastline of east Asia should be drawn. As Nunn demonstrated, the shape in Figure 5 conforms remarkably to the modern map, which he took as confirmation of Bartholomew's skill as a marine surveyor and cartographer (Nunn 1952:13). This suggests strongly that Zorzi indeed had a map, or sketch, from Bartholomew showing this part of the world.

Just how much of the newly discovered region Bartholomew's lost map might have shown cannot be known. It seems reasonable to hypothesize that it showed only the waters and coastlines traversed during the fourth voyage. This is supported by Zorzi's mention of Veragua in the *Informatione* while relating how he obtained his information. That leaves the rest of the maplets to Zorzi, and to this extent Bigelow may well have been correct in assigning the concept of the world they portray to Zorzi, not to the Columbus brothers. That they nevertheless contain some element of their thought is shown by Zorzi's legend on Figure 7, demonstrating the various longitudes favored by Columbus, Marinus, and Ptolemy. The data were available to Zorzi in the *Lettera* (facsimile and translation in Thacher 1903-4 v.2:673, 687).

If this reconstruction is correct, the Columbian inputs were Batholomew's data on Asia-Central America and the information in the legend of Figure 7. With information from the original of the *Informatione*, Zorzi drew the Asian-Central American part of Figure 6. Later, he drew Figure 5, incorporating the shape of the western land provided by Bartholomew, presumably by way of his map. The data on longitudes from the *Lettera* provided the framework for Figures 6 and 7.

Thus Nunn was correct in maintaining that the maplets reflect Columbian ideas, but Bigelow was correct in attributing to Zorzi the major hand in their creation. Sale's unconsidered refutation of any Columbian influence may be discounted.

We return now to the major thesis of this chapter, that on the fourth voyage Columbus believed himself to be on the coast of Asia, and that he died believing this. "Columbus never discovered his error; or, possibly, we should say that it was never proved to him that he was in error" (p. 77). This narrower view has been expanded in a large literature to include discussion of Columbus' initial objective as well as his conclusions about where he had been on all of the voyages. Also, Nunn's conclusion that the major purpose of the fourth voyage was to find a strait leading to the Indian Ocean and India has generated much further discussion, the latest by Taviani (1991:221-225). Here I can address only the former: how has subsequent scholarship dealt with the question of Columbus' belief about what he had reached?

Nunn continued his support of the Asian thesis throughout the rest of his work. He reiterated it at length in 1932 and again, for the last time, in 1952. In 1932 he discussed how subsequent voyagers and conquistadors retained the belief that they were discovering and operating in parts of Asia. This perspective gained acceptance by many scholars, and has been expressed most recently by Stevens, who also demonstrated how the concept of America as Asia was eventually abandoned (Stevens 1989).

Others have concluded that in South America Columbus thought he had discovered a non-Asian part of the world. In the most recent discussion, Sale insisted that Columbus indeed realized that he had found "another world." The idea, originating with Ferdinand, that on the fourth voyage Columbus searched for a strait leading to the Indian Ocean was, according to Sale, accepted by "more gullible historians such as Morison" (Sale 1989:12).

So the discussion continues. Pending further scholarship, perhaps the best hypothesis is that Columbus believed that he had reached Asia while sailing amongst the Caribbean islands and coasting Central America, *and* that he had discovered a new part of the world in South America.

"THE IDENTITY OF 'FLORIDA' ON THE CANTINO MAP OF 1502"

This title would seem to indicate a separate study, but Nunn weaves the question intricately into his main concern: Columbus's objective in sailing westward and what he thought he found. His conclusion, that the strip of "mainland" at the extreme left of the Cantino map represents not Florida, but a part of Asia, did not terminate the debate, which as he pointed out at length (pp. 91-108) had started long before.

Nunn felt the need to reiterate and expand the discussion in 1932. He offered extensive commentary on the contributions of Ptolemy, Marco Polo and Behaim to the concept of the world, including a demonstration that they considered Greenland to be part of Asia. He then continued his thesis that the landmass to the west of Cuba on the Cantino and other maps was meant to represent a part of Asia. "The Canerio [now called Caveri, the next known manuscript map showing part of the New World] and Cantino map makers had no reason to reject the Ptolemy-Marco Polo-Behaim concept on the basis of any discoveries that had been made. That they regarded Greenland as Asia has been shown." A legend at Greenland on the Cantino map ends, " . . . following the opinions of cosmographers, it is believed to be the extremity of Asia" (Nunn's translation, 1932:31). Further, "That the Cantino and Canerio map makers did not conceive of Asia terminating its east coast at this place is proved by the sharp bend of the coast into the edge of the map and by the Greenland legend.[6] Therefore the rest of the Ptolemy-Marco Polo-Behaim Asia must be that portion of the trans-atlantic lands represented by the supposed 'Florida' called *Terra de Cuba Asie Partis* on the Waldseemüller 1516 Carta Marina" (Nunn 1932:52-53).

Penrose, who was not particularly concerned with this issue, commented briefly, " . . . in the Cantino and Canerio maps . . . the existence of Florida is suggested . . . " (Penrose 1952:247). True entered more deeply into the discussion, but also used cautious language: "The Cantino Map of 1502 seems to be the first of a succession of maps of the same design that appear to portray Florida" (True 1954:77).

[6]Nunn did not reproduce the maps in their entirety. Maps in Nebenzahl 1990 illustrate this and many other points made by Nunn as well as those of other scholars cited. Also, they are more legible than was possible in *Geographical Conceptions*.

The next participant was Roukema (1965), who picked up and elaborated on the old suggestion (see Harrisse 1969:80) that what Cantino and others meant to portray was the Yucatán Peninsula. To my knowledge this has not been disproved categorically; it is often listed among the possibilities by scholars who although commenting on the Cantino map did not enter the debate (*e.g.*, Cortesão and Teixeira da Mota, Cumming *et al.*, and Harley, all cited below). However, Morison poked some fun at the idea: " . . . in order to believe that it represents Yucatan you have to twist that peninsula sideways, place it on the wrong side of Cuba—and find a pre-1503 discoverer" (Morison 1974:275).

Caraci took the matter more seriously. He began his commentary with a summary of Nunn's thesis, then proceeded to negate True's. He ended noncommittally: "So far we have been content to show negatively the inadmissibility of True's thesis. We have still to see what solution can be and must be given to the problem of the disputed land mass sketched in to the east [*sic*, for west] of Cuba in the maps we have been examining. But the problem demands a special study, which we will postpone to another occasion" (Caraci 1960:39).

I have not determined that Caraci returned to the subject; if he did, it is not reflected in the subsequent literature I have been able to examine. Comment by Cortesão and Teixeira da Mota was brief, reviewing some pre-1924 opinions and citing Nunn's, but also mentioning the Florida thesis (Cortesão and Teixeira da

Mota 1960-1962 v. 1:10). Hoffman devoted himself more extensively to the question, rejecting the "unrecorded discovery" idea of Harrisse and others as well as the notion that the landmass reflects a discovery by Amerigo Vespucci. He cited Nunn and summarized briefly his idea that "this mainland configuration was, in fact, a confused representation of Cuba; and that this confusion arose from the nature of the source: materials then available on the Columbus voyages. It is easy to see how this might have come about." Hoffman also mentioned briefly the Yucatán, Cuba, and Florida notions, as well as the possibility that the "mainland . . . [was] entirely imaginary." After a long and involved discussion, Hoffman " . . . [found] no basis in fact for a Vespucian origin of the 'Florida' configuration . . . " and agreed with Nunn that Harrisse's solution was found wanting (Hoffman 1961:37, 46, 51).

Wroth discussed at length the knowledge of North America that Giovanni da Verrazzano might have possessed before his voyage of 1524. Among things Verrazzano may have seen on maps was the "triangular peninsula" derived from the Cantino. Wroth traced the feature from the Cantino through Caveri to Waldseemüller 1507, noting that the latter "transmitted the features of both [Cantino and Caveri] to an impressive list of maps, globes, and globe gores reaching to 1520 and beyond." One of these, the Waldseemüller 1516 (*Carta Marina Navigatoria Portugallen Navigationes* . . .), has on the western landmass the name *Terra de Cuba Asie Partis*, which Nunn had noted in support of his thesis (Nunn 1932:53). Wroth considered the phrase and the landmass on the Waldseemüller 1516 an aberrant "regression to the Columbian conception of Cuba as part of the continent." The phrase occurs on the "landmass which Cantino had not named but which he thought of, in all probability, as part of a new continent entirely separated from Asia." Thus, rather off-handedly, Wroth expressed his preference among the various concepts (Wroth 1970: 47-51).

If anyone could present a convincing case, one would think it would be the impressive combination of Cumming, Skelton and Quinn. But their discussion begins, "The most baffling problem on the Cantino map, and on a whole series of later maps, is the identification of a large unnamed landmass placed to the north-west of 'Yssabella,' presumably the island of Cuba." Yucatán and duplication of Cuba are considered briefly. Then, "A third explanation is that it is Florida . . . [which] on the basis of present evidence, appears to be the most reasonable." But then comes the objection that unrecorded voyages must be invoked, and "The problem remains tantalizingly unresolved." Their final comment is that "There are honest confessions of ignorance [regarding the landmass] in such legends as 'Ulterius Terra Incognita'; confusion with Asia or Cuba; strange names such as 'Zoanamela'; and identification with the fabled isle of Bimini" (Cumming *et al.* 1972: 56). "Zoanamela" was explained adequately by Harrisse as a printer's error that found its way onto a map in Gregory Reisch's *Margarita Philosophica*, Strasburg, 1515 (Harrisse 1969:313-314). "Bimini" first appears as "isla de Beimeni" on a landmass north of Cuba on the woodcut map in some copies of Pietro Martire de Angheira's 1511 edition of his "Decades." (For most recent commentary on this map, see Tilton 1989).

Morison was for once noncommittal: " . . . the controversial feature of this chart [Cantino], one which has driven historians and geographers almost frantic, is the continental area jutting out from the western border . . . " He gave Nunn the most space in his discussion, but disagreed on some points of nomenclature, for example: *"Rio de don Diego* might be named after Columbus' older son, the one who stayed at home; *Rio de los Largatos* [sic] might be any river full of nasty alligators. But there is no name or configuration that you can identify with Columbus's voyage along Cuba's south shore." Morison notes that he had suggested previously that the peninsula might have been discovered by Duarte Pacheco Pereira in 1498, or by "some other mariner who reported to him." Then, having entered the lists, he withdrew abruptly: "There I leave the question. Some day, no doubt, an historian more clever than myself will unlock the secret of Cantino's mysterious land" (Morison 1974:275).

In his beautifully produced work on America in old maps, Klemp noted the speculation about the identity of the landmass in the mind of the maker of Cantino's map. Yucatán and a duplicated Cuba are mentioned; then, "Nowadays it is generally assumed to be Florida, with the Key and Pine [?] islands offshore in the south" (Klemp 1976:map 2).

Comment by Schwartz and Ehrenberg was even briefer. The label for the Cantino map says, "First map to present Florida as a peninsula" (Schwartz and Ehrenberg 1980:21).

McGuirk seems to have resolved a confusing issue by demonstrating that the "island" with scroll taken to represent the landmass on the Ruysch 1507 map was designated originally as Cuba. Before printing, "Cuba" was erased from the plate. This supports the opinion that mapmakers were confused about how to portray the new discoveries (McGuirk 1986, 1989a, 1989b).

The last two knowledgeable commentators expressed accurately the present situation regarding Nunn's question. Neither was concerned beyond explicating the Cantino map's place in a sequence that elucidated Columbus's discoveries or the Columbian encounter. The former is Nebenzahl, who in his beautiful and scholarly "Atlas of Columbus" reviewed very briefly the questions about "perhaps the greatest unsolved cartographic puzzle of the period," but offered no solution (Nebenzahl 1990:34). Harley was equally noncommittal, offering only that "This landmass has been the subject of much debate: it may be Yucatan, or even, though improbably, Florida, though there is no surviving record of a landfall in Florida before 1513 or in Yucatan before 1517" (Harley 1990:63).

And there it stands. Nunn thought it was important, and so did many other scholars before and after publication of *Geographical Conceptions*. It is somewhat remindful of the "Columbus landfall" problem—an immense amount of scholarship devoted to a relatively restricted theme in the whole panoply of the effort to understand Columbus and the events and consequences of early European voyages and discoveries.

CONCLUSION

This essay has shown that some of Nunn's work has not survived the scrutiny of other scholars. Serious doubt was cast on the thesis that Columbus verified empirically his measure of $56\frac{2}{3}$ Italian miles in a degree. He did not respond with further arguments; he merely reiterated his original analysis where relevant in further work. However, this did not refute his main contention, that Columbus' use of this erroneous measure influenced his view of the world. It supported the possibility of a relatively short crossing of the Western Ocean.

What did Columbus know about winds and currents in the farther reaches of the Atlantic Ocean before 1492? This is another important matter that remains unresolved. The opinions most opposed to Nunn's were expressed by experienced seamen (and if I may inject my own opinion as a former blue-water sailor, I concur), and even Morison, who held Columbus's skills as navigator and seaman in high regard, did not agree that foreknowledge of the best sailing routes was possible.

Nunn's original ideas about the "Bartholomew Columbus maplets" had to be changed due to cogent criticism by Bigelow and Almagià. With characteristic careful analysis, he acknowledged that the maplets were not in their entirety the work of Bartholomew, but remained convinced that as a whole they reflected the Columbian view. If the maplets did not reflect that view, Nunn's conclusions lost considerable support. Critical to this issue is the independent contribution of Zorzi, a point that could still be argued. It is obvious that Zorzi had sufficient materials at hand from both Christopher and Bartholomew, and Nunn was correct to the extent that Zorzi converted those materials successfully to map form. The matter of Zorzi's dependence on Roselli, or vice versa, remains to be settled.

The possibility of closure for the subjects of the last two chapters seems remote, which leaves none of the problems undertaken by Nunn resolved to everyone's satisfaction. However, at a time when few scholars had ventured much beyond stereotyped versions of the Columbus world view, Nunn essayed a very detailed and at times highly technical as well as original explication. This is the main contribution of *Geographical Conceptions*, a point masked somewhat by the impression given by the chapter titles that the work comprises four separate studies.

In the final analysis, none of the conclusions offered for the four basic questions was accepted uncritically, and some have not stood the test of time. But they had the great value of prompting much debate and further research, and modern scholars regard as still important the subjects treated by Nunn in 1924.

Acknowledgments

Very helpful in the preparation of this essay were Roman Drazniowsky, Curator, American Geographical Society Collection; Susan Peschel and Sharon Hill, AGSC Staff; Jeane Knapp, Golda Meir Library; and Damon Anderson, Research Assistant provided by the Center for Latin America, University of Wisconsin-Milwaukee. Arthur Holzheimer kindly provided a photocopy of his oval map by Roselli showing the part of the east Asian coast that contains the Columbus toponyms. I thank Mary Lynne Bird, Executive Director of the American Geographical Society, for the invitation to participate in the Society's commemoration of the Quincentenary. My participation was encouraged and supported by Peter Watson-Boone, Director of the Golda Meir Library, University of Wisconsin-Milwaukee. This essay is dedicated to the memory of Carl O. Sauer and Erhard Rostlund.

Other Relevant Works by George E. Nunn

1925   "A Reported Map of Columbus," *The Geographical Review*, v. 15, 688-690.

1927   "The Lost Globe Gores of Johann Schöner, *The Geographical Review* v. 17, no. 3, July, pp. 476-480.

1928   *World Map of Francesco Roselli*, Philadelphia: Privately printed.

1928a   Review [& refutation] of Luis Ulloa, *Christophe Colomb, Catalan; la Vrai Genèse de la Découverte de l'Amérique*, Paris: Maisonneuve, 1927, in *American Historical Review*, v. 33, p. 918.

1929   *The Origin of the Strait of Anian Concept.* Philadelphia: Privately printed.

1932   *The Columbus and Magellan Concepts of South American Geography.* Glenside, Pennsylvania: Privately printed.

1933   *Antonio Salamanca's Version of Mercator's Map of 1538 in G. H. Bean's Library.* Cited in *Imago Mundi*, v. 3, p. 15.

1934   *The Mappemonde of Juan de la Cosa*, Jenkintown, Pennsylvania: Privately printed.

1935   "The Imago Mundi and Columbus," *American Historical Review*, v. 40, pp. 646-661.

1937   "Marinus of Tyre's Place in the Columbus Concepts," *Imago Mundi*, v. 2, pp. 27-35.

1946   *The La Cosa Map and the Cabot Voyages. Was New York Bay Discovered by John Cabot, 1498?* [Tall Tree Library, no. 19], Jenkintown, Pennsylvania: Privately printed.

1948   *The Diplomacy Concerning the Discovery of America* [Tall Tree Library, no. 20], Jenkintown, Pennsylvania: Privately printed.

1952   "The Three Maplets Attributed to Bartholomew Columbus," *Imago Mundi*, v. 9, pp. 12-22.

REFERENCES

Almagià, Roberto, 1936, *Intorno a Quattro Codici Fiorentini e ad uno Ferrarese dell'Erudito Veneziano Alessandro Zorzi*, Firenze: Leo S. Olschki.

Almagià, Roberto, 1951, "On the Cartographic Work of Francesco Rosselli," *Imago Mundi*, v. 8, pp. 27-34.

Bigelow, John, 1925, Review of *Geographical Conceptions* in *The American Historical Review*, v. 30, no. 3, April, pp. 601-603.

Bigelow, John, 1935, "The So-called Bartholomew Columbus Map of 1506," *The Geographical Review*, v. 25, no. 4, October, pp. 643-656.

Caraci, Giuseppe, 1960, "The Reputed Inclusion of Florida in the Oldest Nautical Maps of the New World," *Imago Mundi*, v. 15, pp. 32-39.

Charlier, Georges A., 1987, "Value of the Mile Used at Sea by Cristobal Colon During His First Voyage," in Gerace, pp. 115-119.

Colección de Documentos para la Historia de Costa Rica Relativos al Cuarto y Ultimo Viaje de Cristóbal Colón, 1952, San José: Atenea.

Cortesão, Armando, and Avelino Teixeira da Mota, 1960-1962, *Portugaliae Monumenta Cartographica*, 6 vols., Lisboa: Comissão Executiva das Commemorações do V Centenario da Morte do Infante D. Henrique.

Cumming, W. P., R. A. Skelton and D. B. Quinn, 1972, *The Discovery of North America*, New York: American Heritage.

Davies, Arthur, 1977, "Behaim, Martellus, and Columbus," *The Geographical Journal*, v. 143, pp. 451-459.

Edwards, Clinton R. and Damon Anderson, 1992, *The Columbus Collection: A Chronological List of Books and Reprints in the American Geographical Society Collection [AGSC Special Publication no. 3*, in preparation].

"E. H.," 1925, Review of *Geographical Conceptions . . .* in *The Geographical Journal*, v. 66, no. 5, November, pp. 465-466.

Gerace, Donald T., comp., 1987, *Columbus and His World*, Fort Lauderdale (Florida): College of the Finger Lakes.

Harley, J. B., 1990, *Maps and the Columbian Encounter*, Milwaukee: University of Wisconsin-Milwaukee, Golda Meir Library.

Harrisse, Henry, 1886, *Bibliotheca Americana Vetustissima*, New York: Geo. P. Philes.

Harrisse, Henry, 1969, *The Discovery of North America*, Amsterdam: N. Israel [originally published 1892].

Hoffman, Bernard G., 1961, *Cabot to Cartier. Sources for a*

Historical Ethnography of Northeastern North America 1497-1550, Toronto: University of Toronto Press.

Kelley, James E., Jr., 1983, "In the Wake of Columbus on a Portolan Chart," *Terrae Incognitae*, v. 15, pp. 77-111.

Kelley, James E., Jr., 1987, "The Navigation of Columbus on His First Voyage to America," in Gerace, 1987, pp. 121-140.

Klemp, Egon, comp. and ed., 1976, *America in Maps Dating from 1500 to 1856*, New York and London: Holmes and Meier.

Laguarda Trias, Rolando A., 1963, "Elucidario de las Latitudes Colombinas," *Boletín de la Real Sociedad Geográfica*, v. 99, pp. 181-245.

Laguarda Trias, Rolando A., 1974, *El Enigma de las Latitudes de Colón*, Valladolid.

Magnaghi, Alberto, 1928, "I Presunti Errori che Vengono Attribuiti a Colombo nella Determinazione delle Latitudini," *Bolletino della Società Geografica Italiana*, v. 65, pp. 459-94, 553-82.

McGuirk, Donald L., Jr., 1986, "The Mystery of Cuba on the Ruysch Map," *The Map Collector*, v. 36, September, pp. 40-41.

McGuirk, Donald L., Jr., 1989a, "The Depiction of Cuba on the Ruysch World Map," *Terrae Incognitae*, v. 20, pp. 89-97.

McGuirk, Donald L., Jr., 1989b, "Ruysch World Map: Census and Commentary," *Imago Mundi*, v. 41, pp. 133-141.

McElroy, Lieutenant John W., 1941, "The Ocean Navigation of Columbus on his First Voyage," *The American Neptune*, v. 1, no. 3, pp. 209-240.

Menander, Captain J., 1926, "The Navigation of Columbus," *Proceedings of the U. S. Naval Institute*, v. 52, pp. 665-673.

Morison, Samuel Eliot, 1941, "Columbus and Polaris," *The American Neptune*, v. 1, no. 1, pp. 6-25; no. 2, pp. 123-37.

Morison, Samuel Eliot, 1974, *The European Discovery of America: The Southern Voyages A.D. 1492-1616*, New York: Oxford University Press.

Morison, Samuel Eliot, 1991 , *Admiral of the Ocean Sea*, 2 v., Norwalk, Connecticut: The Easton Press [originally published 1942].

Nebenzahl, Kenneth, 1990, *Atlas of Columbus and The Great*

Discoveries, Chicago: Rand McNally.

Nowell, Charles, 1939, "The Columbus Question: A Survey of Recent Literature and Present Opinion," *The American Historical Review*, v. 44, no. 4, July.

Nunn, George E., see separate bibliography, p. 190.

Penrose, Boies, 1952, *Travel and Discovery in the Renaissance*, Cambridge, Massachusetts: Harvard University Press.

[Postille, 1892-96] "Postille alla 'Historia Rerum Ubique Gestarum' di Pio II," *Raccolta*, Part I, v. 2, no. 860.

Raccolta di Documenti e Studi Pubblicati dalla R. Commissione Colombiana . . . , 6 parts in 14 vols., Roma.

Ramos, Demetrio, 1988, *O Alcance das Viagens de Colombo para o Domínio do Atlântico*, Lisboa: Instituto de Investigação Científica Tropical. [Text in Spanish].

Randles, W. G. L., 1990, "The Evaluation of Columbus' 'India' Project by Portuguese and Spanish Cosmographers in the Light of the Geographical Science of the Period," *Imago Mundi*, v. 42, pp. 50-64.

Roukema, E., 1965, "A Discovery of Yucatan Prior to 1503," *Imago Mundi*, v. 13, pp. 30-38.

Sale, Kirkpatrick, 1989, "What Columbus Died Believing: The *True* Geographic Concepts of the Great Discoverer," *Terrae Incognitae*, v. 21, pp. 9-16.

Schwartz, Seymour and Ralph E. Ehrenberg, 1980, *The Mapping of America*, New York: Harry N. Abrams.

Stevens, Errol Wayne, 1989, "The Asian-American Connection: The Rise and Fall of a Cartographic Idea," *Terrae Incognitae*, v. 21, pp. 27-39.

Taviani, Paolo Emilio, 1991. *Columbus. The Great Adventure*, translated by Luciano R. Farina and Marc A. Beckwith, New York: Orion.

Taylor, E. G. R., 1952, "The Navigating Manual of Columbus," *Journal of the Institute of Navigation*, v. 5, no. 1, January, pp. 42-54.

Thacher, John Boyd, 1903-4, *Christopher Columbus: His Life, His*

Work His Remains, 3 vols., New York and London: G. P. Putnam's Sons.

Tilton, David W., 1989, "Yucatán on the Peter Martyr Map?," *Terrae Incognitae*, v. 21, pp. 17-25.

True, David O., 1954, "Some Early Maps Relating to Florida," *Imago Mundi*, v. 11, pp. 73-84.

[Varela, 1984] Colón, Cristóbal, *Textos y Documentos Completos*, edición, prólogo y notas de Consuelo Varela, Madrid: Alianza Editorial.

Wieser, Fr. R. von, 1893, "Karte des Bartolomeo Colombo über die vierte Reise des Admirals," reprint from *Mitteilungen des Instituts für österr. Geschichtsforschung*, Ergänzungsband IV. Innsbruck: Wagner'schen Universitäts-Buchhandlung.

Wroth, Lawrence C., 1970, *The Voyages of Giovanni da Verrazzano, 1524-1528*, New Haven and London: Yale University Press.

Zorzi, Alessandro, n.d., ["*Lettera Rarissima*"], manuscript, Classe XIII, Cod. 81, Biblioteca Nazionale Centrale de Firenze. (Facsimile and transcription in Thacher, 1903-4, v. 2, pp. 669-699.)

Zorzi, Alessandro, [1504?], *Informatiō di Bart° Colōbo della navicatiō di ponēte et garbī di Beragna nel mondo nouo 15*[illegible]*4*, manuscript, B. R. (Banco Raro) 234, ff. 31r-34v, Biblioteca Nazionale Centrale de Firenze. (Transcribed with modernized orthography in Harrisse, 1866, pp. 471-474 and reproduced in *Colección*, 1952, pp. 72-74.)